the Pieced Quilt

the Pieced Quilt

an American Design Tradition

Jonathan Holstein

New York Graphic Society
Boston, Massachusetts

Endpapers: Appliqué quilt, c. 1895. Made by Mrs. Harriet Powers of
Athens, Georgia. 105″ x 69″. A story-telling or ''scene'' appliqué quilt.
Mrs. Powers mixed her interpretations of Biblical stories with local
events of significance to her. (Courtesy of Boston Museum of Fine Arts)

Frontispiece: Broken Star, Carpenter's Wheel, or Dutch Rose.
Pennsylvania, dated 1887. Cotton. 82″ x 79½″. See plate 22.

Dedication page: Schoolhouse. Pennsylvania, c. 1900. 84″ x 80″.
This quilt's fine graphic qualities overcome its grounding in Victorian
nostalgia. The design extracts the essentials of the country schoolhouse:
walls, roof, windows, door—and chimneys. (Rhea Goodman,
Quilt Gallery, Inc.)

A NOTE ON THE PLATES

While in the text I have attempted to deal in a comprehensive manner with the whole
subject of American pieced quilts, the selection of plates is more personal. It
does not reflect an effort to show the most typical examples, but rather those we
could find which were to us most visually interesting, which seemed to make a
cohesive, valid, and distinct visual statement, representing an authentic aesthetic
problem posed and resolved. Thus we have neglected craft (though most are
well-made) to concentrate on design; we have applied the same standards one
would to a judgment of paintings or other objects of visual importance. It is not
technical facility which makes aesthetic objects work, but that masterful
comprehension of form and its sure joining to line and color which gives the viewer
a sense of being in the presence of an important, moving, and complete visual
statement. In few cases is it possible to establish positively the provenance of these
quilts; in the captions, all that is indicated by the state is the place where the quilt was
found. All dimensions given in the captions are in inches; height precedes width.

All quilts, unless otherwise noted, are in the Gail van der Hoof/
Jonathan Holstein collection.

International Standard Book Number: 0-8212-0534-10 (cloth)
International Standard Book Number: 0-8212-0686-9 (paper)
Library of Congress Catalog Card Number: 73-79991

First paperback printing 1975

Designed by Betsy Beach

New York Graphic Society books are published by Little, Brown and Company.

Manufactured in the United States of America

For Gail

1 Introduction

This is a book about American pieced quilts, the kind whose tops are made from pieces of material sewn together, usually in geometric patterns. I must state at the outset that it is a very personal view of these objects: I am interested more in their visual content than their craft.

Obviously, the two cannot be divorced; the hand of the creator is always proudly, sometimes triumphantly, there. And I admire completely the superb needlework many of these quilts display. Such handwork is an integral part of the quilt's place in the American pastoral legend. Quilts are token of our pre-industrial past, the homestead which exists in fact or myth, and the hand skills which our ancestors practiced as a matter of course, symbolic of virtuous household industry. Industrialization has made us acutely aware of the monetary value of time units; labor is sold in short time spans which can be conveniently rationalized with production cost factors. We have noticed two common reactions when people examine a superbly made and intricately stitched quilt: "How did she find time to do it?" (She had to, so she did.) And: "I wouldn't do that for . . ," and some figure is named, indicating their feeling that such work no doubt took hours, days, perhaps months, and the monetary value they would attach to such extended labor. It is a practical consideration; for many fewer hours of work they could earn the money to buy a bedcover fully as efficient. No such analysis was made by the women who made quilts. They were extremely proud of the time and effort which went into the more elaborate examples. Women counted the number of spools of thread that went into a quilt; the more spools, the better—though in terms of function it would have been better not to quilt it down so lavishly. Fine work was prized; they were making an object to be shown and used with pride, a conspicuous example of their feminine skills. There was obviously great personal satisfaction in quiltmaking. Early accounts speak eloquently of the great pleasure women had in turning to their quilting at the end of laborious pioneer days. Long after sewing machines were ubiquitous in American life, quilts continued to be made by hand. Many still are, though they don't need to be. The presence of a machine-run edge, the long and boring finish of a quilt, as the only element of mechanical work in a great quilt a century

Figure 3. Variable Star. Pennsylvania, c. 1855. Cotton. 87" x 87". See plate 18.

or more old, speaks eloquently of the presence of the machine in the next room, or at a neighbor's house, and the choice to use it only sparingly.

Old hand ways go as machines are invented to do the same job, or are eliminated when society no longer values or needs them. As industrial culture has expanded outward, becoming ever more inclusive and committed to continual innovation, the hand-based skills of an earlier, more stable and static time become less significant in an economic analysis, but perhaps more meaningful emotionally as relics of a "simpler" age. So I think it is not only the critical faculties in us which respond to those stitches practiced as a matter of course by our ancestors—it is almost certainly the romantic. We are impressed by those needlework triumphs because most of us wouldn't do them; it is not that we couldn't.

If we strip away, then, the awe of handwork, much the awe of the sophisticate for the practical knowledge of the country or the skills of a previous time, and if we put aside the romantic associations of the quilt in American life, we can begin perhaps to see them in a different but equally meaningful way. And that, simply, is what we have tried to do.

For that leaves us with surface, with pattern, color, and form. And here the word "American" becomes important. Pieced quilts of great workmanship, great "craft," were made in other places, though few. But it was in America that they became a design phenomenon of great interest and, I believe, of singular importance. If we neglect the stitches, it is only to concentrate on an equally great accomplishment, one in which the makers took equal pride: their beauty from a distance, seen opened and proudly spread like paintings on the family beds. To do this we have had, symbolically and actually, to take them from the setting of the bedroom and to hang them on the wall. It could be argued that this is making of quilts something that they were not intended to be, making them into "paintings." Yet the woman who conceived a quilt saw it in her mind open and similarly "on a wall"—otherwise she could not have envisioned it. Sometimes it was sketched first, precisely laid out. Always it was planned, and with rare exceptions, planned completely. You will not be able to see, in many cases, the pattern or quality of the quilting stitches in the plates. Nor, do I think, did the woman who planned it see those stitches in her mind, except as the lines of quilting would create a dimensional effect she might have foreseen. What she saw was precisely those patterns of color and form which one can see in a photograph of the opened quilt. In fact, in terms of design, this is perhaps truer to her original graphic insight and plan than the finished quilt falling in sections over a bed.

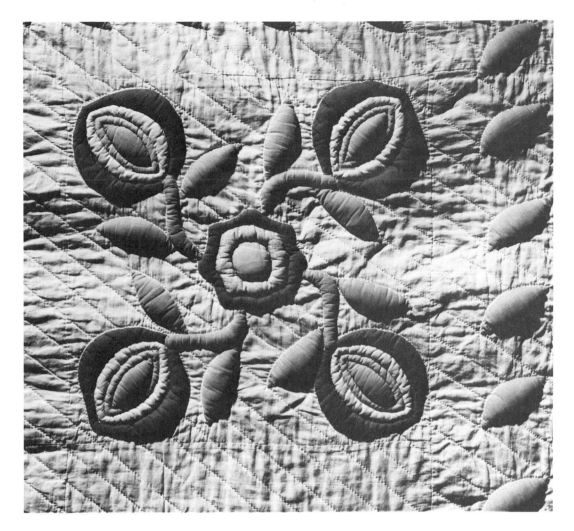

Figure 4. Stuffed Pomegranate. Pennsylvania, c. 1860. Cotton. One section of a stuffed quilt, showing the Pomegranate design. The design was cut out and appliquéd to a top; threads beneath the appliquéd parts on the back of the top were carefully parted, and little bits of cotton added until the design was fully stuffed.

There were a number of compelling reasons for taking this approach to quilts. One was my feeling that an important body of American design had been largely overlooked. Another was the sure knowledge that thousands of these objects were being put to mean uses and destroyed every year, before anyone had had a chance to evaluate their significance; I hope to prompt more caution in dealing with them. A final reason was my feeling that little attempt had been made, in all of the books on the subject, to deal directly with the history and aesthetics of pieced quilts, to separate the romance from what factual material existed, and to formulate, if possible, a reasonable theory of why they were made, where the impetus for creating these strong designs came from, why it persisted for such a long period. I wanted to answer these questions both by dealing with the technique and by taking a long-range view of their surfaces rather than a close-up of their stitches.

This is not, however, to divorce these quilts from their function, for that is an important part of their being. A quilt has to do with protection. It is a cloth sand-

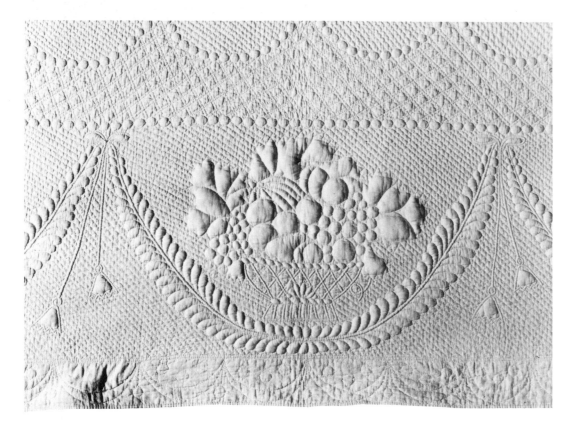

Figure 5. A detail of a finely quilted and stuffed plain white quilt, showing the elaboration which was possible in this type. (America Hurrah Antiques, N.Y.C.)

wich, with a top, usually the decorated part, a back, and a filler in between. The term comes from the Latin *culcita,* meaning a stuffed sack. It has come to be both a noun, the bed quilt, and a verb, to quilt, which means simply the act of stitching through the three layers to hold them together. The filler is always a material with bulk and resilience—most anciently, perhaps, leaves, grass, feathers; now, cotton, wool, the synthetics, all in batting form. It is a craft which has produced many things besides bed quilts: padding under metal armor and light armor itself, decorative clothing and underclothing, curtains, and so on. Almost always its purpose is protection: against blows, as in armor; against heat or cold, as in pot holders and sleeping bags; layered materials are very efficient at this. Its application to bed furnishings has been in quilts for the bed itself and curtains which surrounded those early "great" bedsteads, to protect against both drafts and cold.

Bed quilts are of three main types: the plain quilt, made of single pieces of material front and back, usually of a single color or printed pattern, and the two types which have been collectively called "patchwork": appliqué quilts, which have tops made of whole cloth to which have been applied—stitched down—forms cut from other cloth of contrasting color; and pieced quilts, which have tops made from pieces of material stitched together mosaic-fashion to form patterns and borders, usually of a geometric nature. Often, and especially in

American pieced quilts, there is a repeated geometric pattern in a series of blocks. These latter two techniques for making quilt tops are the application of other ancient decorative textile methods to the quilt. During the medieval period, pieced and appliqué techniques were widely used to make or decorate, among other things, clothing, banners, and military cloaks, and there is surviving evidence of appliqué work almost 3,000 years old. In the plain quilt, the decorative effects come primarily from the textural patterns created by the compression of the filler by the quilting stitches. Almost always the patterns are carefully planned, and can be gorgeously elaborate and intricate. At the same time, the plain quilt can be the most rudimentary, made for utility only, and simply "tufted" or tied through in enough places to keep the filling from shifting and bunching. Covers are also made of two layers of material stitched together but with no stuffing between; because they use the same basic techniques and employ the same decorative effects as the more common three-layered quilts, lacking only the filler, they are also classified as quilts. Sometimes they are called "summer" quilts in obvious reference to their use as a lighter bedcover for the more temperate seasons.

The normal method of making pieced or appliqué quilts is first to design and finish a top. Then a quilting frame, resembling a large picture frame, is set up. It rests flat, either on supports such as saw horses, legs, or four chair backs, or is suspended from the ceiling; the first was the arrangement more preferred in the Northeast, the latter is more typical of the South. There is space for four or more quilters to sit around it. The material chosen for the quilt back is attached to the frame, the filler spread evenly over, then the top is stretched over all, and the three layers are quilted, stitched through, following lines drawn on the top. When the quilting is completed, the sides are finished either by stitching surplus material at the edges of the top and back together, or by bringing either the top or back material over the other and stitching it down, or by running a binding around both.

Before leaving this introduction I would like to make a few terms explicit. "Patchwork" has traditionally meant, in England and the United States, both "appliqué" and "pieced" work with emphasis on the latter. I prefer and will use "pieced" for that technique, because it is more explicit and avoids otherwise necessary modifiers ("mosaic," as in "mosaic patchwork" is the most common). I will use "patchwork" only in its traditional sense, inclusive of both appliqué and pieced techniques. I will also use the word "block-style" as a term to describe that method of quilt-top construction in which repeating designs, usually geometric, are assembled first in identical "blocks" and then pieced together, a method particularly popular among American quiltmakers.

2 The Background of Patchwork

Early man, to blunt the wind and conserve body heat, no doubt added the protective, insulating, hairy skins of other animals to his own relatively thin one. It was a natural, direct solution. With the animal's skin against his own and the hair out, it acted as a "blanket." With the hair in, the animal skin became, in effect, an unstitched quilt—his skin and the animal's forming the two outer layers, the hair between, the insulating medium. An attempt to make a softer bed by piling up such organic materials as leaves and branches to sleep on, with or without skins top and bottom, served a double purpose: evening off and padding out the ground, and providing an insulating layer against the earth's chill. The next logical development, that of stuffing a sewn bag or carefully flensed whole animal skin with filler to make a mattress, was no doubt taken at a very early date. When the final step was taken—sewing or tieing the sack through to keep the filler from shifting and bunching—making a quilt—is of course impossible to determine; but the form is certainly of great antiquity. And when the mattress went on top to become a "quilt" is equally a matter of conjecture; one assumes that the insulating properties of the stuffed sack—a form which persists in the featherbed of Northern Europe were recognized simultaneously with its advent as a mattress.

By the time quilts appear in written records they are in the modern form in terms of technique, and would have had woven materials top and bottom with a filler of wool, down, or perhaps cotton in between. The distinction between mattress and cover was noted in an English will of 1477 which lists "unum fedderbed" and "unum twylt."[1]

In the East quilts seem to have been used both as bedding and floor carpets. Perhaps the earliest surviving example of quilted work is that carpet preserved in the Leningrad Department of the Institute of Archaeology of the Academy of Sciences in Russia, which was found in a tomb of 100 B.C.–200 A.D. It is decorated with quilting stitches in geometric motifs and animals in the Scythian style, and likely served as a floor piece; it was so placed in the tomb.[2]

The earliest surviving quilts of European manufacture are three famous Sicilian pieces of the early fifteenth century, all showing scenes from the legend of

Figure 6. Broderie perse quilt. America, c. 1800. Cotton. 96" x 90". The figures in this appliqué quilt were cut from English chintz of the late eighteenth century. The broderie perse technique developed after the arrival of Indian chintzes in Europe; the chintzes were characterized by finely detailed color figures suitable for such work. (Ginsburg & Levy)

Tristan and Iseult. They are made of coarse linen, the figures outlined in linen thread and stuffed out trapunto-fashion. Almost certainly there had been local manufacture of quilts in Europe before the first written records appear. That only three specimens have survived is not surprising. Quilts used by common people were no doubt of hardy materials, such as linen and wool, but were simply worn out. The more sumptuous fabrics, silks and velvets, used by people of means, were even less likely to stand the passage of time.

What relatively scanty references there are to quilts before the end of the medieval period are to be found in literature and household accounts. There is an early reference in *Les Lais del Desiré,* a collection of French poems of the twelfth or thirteenth century, to what is unmistakably a patchwork quilt: "The bed was prepared of which the quilt was of a check-board pattern of two sorts of silk cloth, well-made and rich."[3] Other references over the next few centuries are not specific enough to tell what sorts of quilts were involved; and whether these early quilts were of domestic European manufacture or imported is impossible to say. That quilts were being imported is certain. There is a record of one coming in a cargo from Brittany to England in 1498–99.[4] And it seems equally certain that fine fabrics, including quilts, were coming from the East and had been for some time.

Domestic production of quilts would have been of three types: common quilts of plain materials whose only purpose was warmth, plain quilts of sumptuous materials made for show and warmth, and quilts of both English and imported materials worked with fine embroidery, largely for show. The English from an early date had a special fondness and aptitude for embroidery. The art ". . . was the favourite pursuit—almost the only accomplishment—of the ladies of the Saxon and Anglo-Norman laity."[5] Ecclesiastical embroidery, done by professionals, flourished for some centuries, reaching a height in the thirteenth century when "opus Anglicum" was treasured throughout the Christian world.

During the fifteenth century there was one practice of interest to us—that of embroidering designs on a ground and then cutting them out and applying them to another fabric, ". . . a comparatively quick way of producing a richly decorated textile."[6] "Applied work had a special appeal for amateurs since it was much easier to decorate a silk or velvet hanging or cushion with small motifs worked separately in linen and afterwards applied than to attempt to embroider directly on to the richer material itself."[7] The emergence of the middle class, a process hastened during the Tudor reign in the sixteenth century, brought with it an increasing demand for decoration to adorn the homes and bodies of both noble and merchant; and with this there came a rise in fine amateur needlework, which often rivaled that of the professional embroiderers. This trend was accentuated

Figure 7. Tree of Life. India, mid-eighteenth century. Palampore. 109″ x 109″. A typical flowering tree palampore. (Collection of Cora Ginsburg)

in the Elizabethan era; the work of amateurs was often on a level of that done by guild members. The Elizabethans loved elaborate work, and as a result their decorated textiles were lush and intricate.

There are many references to quilts in the sixteenth century.[8] Quilts seem to have been made of all materials, but those in inventories lean more toward fine textiles, particularly silk, most likely because these were considered of sufficient value to be recorded.

Early European fabrics were largely wool, linen, and silk. Cotton was a foreign crop, and what cotton goods were used were imported, although not in any great quantity prior to the Elizabethan period. Starting in the sixteenth century, however, England imported quantities of cotton fabrics from India, and this was to have major implications for the development of pieced quilts. The Indian cotton or chintzes were much sought after because of the permanence of their

Figure 8. Linen bedspread embroidered in red and yellow silk, and quilted. England, first half of eighteenth century. The central-medallion style with similar matching corners influenced patchwork quilt design. (Courtesy of Victoria and Albert Museum)

color; India had many centuries earlier mastered the art of mordant dyeing.[9] The system of mordant dyeing was laborious, painstaking, and ingenious; a large piece was at least a month in the making, and required an extraordinary number of different hand steps. If indigo was wanted in the design, the textile also had to go through a process of resist dyeing, using waxes. It should be remembered that only the finest Indian textiles were made this way, the designs painted on by master craftsmen. The bulk was much cheaper cloths, in which the mordants were applied with printing blocks rather than by the skilled hand of a textile painter. Nevertheless, both types were traded far and wide and it was the permanence and brilliance of their colors that created a demand lasting hundreds of years. Compared to them, European printed and painted fabrics of the period were poor indeed, the colors limited and impermanent; for, in fact, they had to learn the secrets of mordant dyeing from the Indians.

Interest in Indian textiles grew slowly but surely in England. The first fabrics no doubt went back as exotic curios, but it was not long before the East India

Figure 9. Central-medallion-style quilt. England, c. 1810. Cotton. The central-medallion style in an English manifestation, retaining appliqué and pieced elements, decorated corners, multiple borders. The central panel was made to commemorate the fiftieth anniversary of George III's accession. (Courtesy of Victoria and Albert Museum)

Company was trying out the commercial possibilities in London.[10] What did the Indian fabrics and the quilts made from them look like? Flowers, plants, vines, animals and human figures were done on backgrounds often of red, the designs in red, blue, green, brown, in the Indian style, or in styles reflecting the tastes of China, Persia, Japan—countries that had been importing Indian textiles for centuries and to whose desires the cotton painters had catered. Some were bordered, as finished scenes; others were yard goods, with repeated smaller figures.

In 1633 Emanuel Altman wrote Thomas Colley, at Petapoli in India, "to have made for him 'six very large lansoles well painted with flowers, big enough for an English bed; also two or three pillow beers. . . .' "[11] In this is the clue to what eventually happened. It was recognized by the Company that popular acceptance could be increased if the designs were more to the English taste. In 1643 the Company auctioned some "Pintado Quilts" in London and was dissatisfied with the results; they wrote to India: ". . . they serve more to content and pleasure our friends than for any profit [that] ariseth in sales. . . . Those which hereafter you shall send we desire may be with more white ground, and the flowers and branch to be in colours in the middle of the quilt as the painter pleases, whereas now the most part of your quilts come with sad red grounds, which are not equally sorted to please all buyers. . . ."[12] Starting in 1662 the Company sent designs tailored to English taste to India, to be reproduced by the textile makers. This tack was successful. Demand for the fabrics grew, and the trade swelled enormously in the next fifty years, concurrent with the increased prosperity at home, more open, gracious houses, and the desire for bright and bold materials to use in them. The practical qualities of Indian fabrics—their durability and color-fastness—made them ideal for both clothes and furnishings.

As time went on, European designs were synthesized and blended with Indian motifs, along with influences from Persia, China, Japan, and the other countries to which India exported textiles. There was an early movement between embroidered and painted designs. (Indian textile makers themselves used the same motifs in both techniques, especially for quilts and palampores, the painted hangings which were also used as bedcovers.) Embroidered and painted chintzes in almost identical designs have survived.[13] Among the designs sent out to India to be copied there were most likely embroidery patterns printed in England in the seventeenth century. A set of chintz hangings and an embroidered palampore of the late seventeenth century, formerly in Ashburnham House in England, have the same design source, which was "probably a printed one published in England for embroideries." Thus there was a continuous cross-fertilization—English embroidery designs incorporated into Indian chintzes, English ladies copying in embroidery Indian chintz designs—with all of the complicated interchange that implies. What is most important is that designs which the English favored or found compatible for decoration were coming in as bold, clean patterns on color-fast materials.

The increasing popularity of these fabrics caused a great uproar. In both France and England domestic manufacturers of textiles, particularly silk and wool, agitated for trade barriers against chintzes. The first such action in England was an act of 1700 which levied a 15 percent duty on imported textiles and outlawed their sale in England after 1701. It had little effect, in part because canny importers marked chintzes for reexport, which was legal, then off-loaded them at quiet sections of the English coast. Daniel Defoe's *Weekly Review* for January 31, 1708, had this to say:

The general fansie of the people runs upon East India goods to that degree that the chintz and painted callicoes, which before were only made use of for car-

pets, quilts, &c, and to cloth children and ordinary people, become now the dress of our ladies; and such is the power of a mode we saw our persons of quality dressed in Indian carpets, which but a few years before then chamber-maids would have thought too ordinary for them: the chints was advanced from lying upon their floors to their backs, from the foot-cloth to the petticoat; and even the queen herself at this time was pleased to appear in China and Japan; I mean China silks and callico. Nor was this all, but it crept into our houses, our closets, and bed-chambers; curtains, cushions, chairs, and at last beds them-selves were nothing but callicoes or Indian stuffs; and in short, almost everything that used to be made of wool or silk, relating either to the dress of the women or the furniture of our houses, was supplied by the Indian trade.[14]

In 1721, therefore, there was passed, "An act to preserve and encourage the Woolen and Silk Manufacturers . . . by prohibiting the Use and Wear of all printed, painted, stained or dyed callicoes in apparel, household stuff, furniture or otherwise after the twenty-fifth day of December, 1722." No one could "ex-pose for sale any printed, painted, stained or dyed callicoe, or any bed, chair, cushion, window curtain or other household stuff or furniture made up or mixed with any printed, painted or stained callico" for use in Great Britain.[15] This pro-hibition had about as much effect as one would imagine. In 1728 Defoe wrote ". . . that the evil of a consumption of Indian manufactures still prevailed," and he ascribed it to a cause for which he saw no remedy—"passion for their fashion."[16]

While the acts ultimately could not stop the flow of materials, the various diffi culties put in the way of trade did keep supplies low for a period, and this is an important factor: people wanted to make the most of their scarce chintzes. A woman left with scraps after cutting up her precious Indian cloth for clothes or domestic furnishings, or with worn-out articles with some good parts left, had two alternatives, aside from throwing them away: either sew the scraps or sal-vaged parts together to make a whole pieced-work textile, or use them for ap-pliqué. The lack of surviving evidence make it at this point very difficult to determine which alternative might have been used first, or if they were used concurrently. The Victoria and Albert Museum's *Guide to English Embroidery,* speaking of the mid-eighteenth century, says:

A technique which assumed prominence at this time was patchwork. Early pieces are usually very simple, consisting of rectangles of printed cottons joined together to make a quilt or coverlet which might be further embellished with simple embroidery. . . . Towards the end of the century there arose a fashion for cutting shapes or motifs out of printed cottons and applying them to a plain ground, a technique often combined with patchwork.[17]

A number of quilts using such a combination of techniques have survived in both England and the United States, and date from the last quarter of the eighteenth century. From the preceding century, however, there is nothing in cotton in either technique.

If, indeed, English needleworkers first used chintzes for pieced work, the progression could have been from large pieces cut into squares and sewn together, to smaller, more complex geometric shapes which could use even the smallest scraps. The inherent decorative possibilities in even small pieces of the boldly patterned chintzes might have prompted housewives to stretch their supply by spacing them out with neutral fabrics in between the chintz pieces. This approach was taken in the earliest surviving pieced cotton quilt. and the only such quilt known using seventeenth-century Indian chintzes: the set of bed furnishings —quilt and hangings—at Levens Hall in Cumberland, which according to family tradition was made in 1708; it certainly appears to date from the early part of the eighteenth century (figure 10). The pieces are cut in octagonal, cruciform, and crystalline shapes and arranged in a regular, repeating pattern; some of them are made up of even smaller pieces put together, an indication that chintz was indeed highly valued, and that this gave an impetus to pieced work. The intervening white sections are pieced together with the chintz forms.

Another progression to the Levens Hall type of work is possible. Given the striking resemblance of many chintz patterns, with their lively colors and finely drawn figures, to traditional embroidery designs, the application of chintz pieces to a neutral ground for hangings or spreads would be a logical development. It would work as a kind of "instant" embroidery, the finished effect from a distance remarkably like the far more time-consuming stitchery. There is evidence that chintz was used as substitute embroidery. Daniel Defoe, literary scourge of domestic folly, wrote of Indian cottons in 1719: ". . . the ladies converted their Carpets and quilts into Gowns and Petticoats and made the broad and uncouth Bordures of the former serve instead of the rich Laces and Embroideries they were used to wear."[18] Also, as we have seen, chintzes made for the English markets were coming through with white grounds. With carefully selected scraps, or the useable parts of worn materials, a woman could have reproduced the general look of a whole piece of chintz—or a chintz quilt—by appliquéing the pieces to a white background.

Figure 10. The earliest example of pieced quilts extant, and the only one using seventeenth-century Indian chintzes, is in a set of bed furnishings in Levens Hall in England. Illustrated are sections of the bed curtains; the quilt is identical. (Collection Levens Hall, Cumberland, England. Photo courtesy of Victoria and Albert Museum)

An effect in appearance even closer to embroidery, and with similar decorative impact, could be achieved by carefully cutting out complete design elements —birds, animals, flowers—from a piece of chintz and sewing them down. (This technique, "broderie perse," which most likely originated in the eighteenth century, survived well into the nineteenth in the United States. So popular was this technique that in the early nineteenth century, chintzes were printed with patterns especially designed to be cut out and used for the centers and corners of appliqué quilts.)

If large scraps could be used, showing fairly complete areas of designs, could not even smaller fragments, with little sections of pattern, be put to some good purpose? They could, of course, be applied to a ground in some agreeable arrangement. This would imply some regular cutting and placement of the pieces so that a harmonious effect would be achieved, and the obvious way to do that is with geometric shapes in an organized pattern. Once such shapes

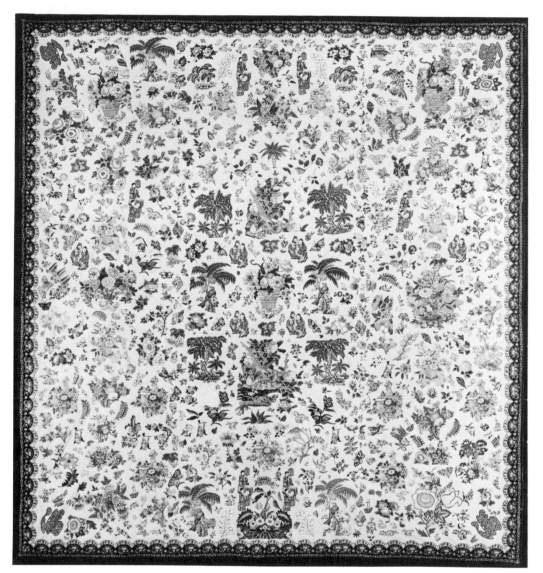

Figure 11. Appliqué coverlet, c. 1800. English chintzes of mid-eighteenth century. 104″ x 98″. The extreme of broderie perse, each piece cut out and painstakingly applied. The design was carefully balanced using many different elements. (Ginsburg & Levy)

were cut out and arranged on a ground, it would be immediately apparent that the open spaces between the printed pieces—the "background"—could also be made from scraps; a regular arrangement of geometric forms on a surface creates, of course, equally regular shapes in between.

Regardless, however, of which technique was first employed, such work was the outcome. The Levens Hall quilt and curtains, while they are themselves pieced in a continual-mosaic method, are the earliest surviving relatives of the American block-style pieced quilt. No American pieced quilt—or quilt of any variety, for that matter—of a comparable age survives; however, that is the only pieced quilt of such an early date which has surfaced in England, and from there, until the last quarter of the eighteenth century, there is nothing in either country. It is unlikely, however, that it was an orphan, and certainly the type had descendants. In the England of 1700, for example, an elderly woman wrote the London *Spectator* "deploring the decay of needlework among young girls," whom she scathingly described as "proud, idle flirts sipping tea for a whole afternoon in a room hung with the industry of their great-grandmothers." She went on to say: "For my part I have plyed my needle these fifty years [since 1650] and by my goodwill would never have it out of my hands. . . . I have quilted counterpanes and chest covers in fine white linen, in various patterns of my own invention. . . . I have made patchwork beyond calculation." [19] Averil Colby points out that Swift had Gulliver describe his clothes as looking ". . . like the patchwork done by the ladies in England, only that mine were all of a color." [20] (*Gulliver's Travels* was published in 1726.) Practically none of what must have been an immense body of patchwork has survived. It is mainly plain imported quilts and those made domestically of fine materials, richly embroidered, which survived in England from the several centuries preceding the nineteenth.

It is improbable that the ladies of Levens Hall invented the system they used in their quilts and hangings; they are too "finished" in the sense of sophisticated technique and design not to have had precursors. It is very possible that pieced work in geometric patterns for quilts and hangings was crafted both by peasant and well-to-do before the arrival of chintzes, and possibly has a very long history in England indeed, the evidence for which, like that for most things made of materials, which tend to be reused until they are of no further use and then discarded, has disappeared. Complicated crafts do not arise spontaneously; all to my knowledge have developed in a logical manner. I believe that among those now-lost covers there might well have been more direct ancestors of the block-style pieced quilt than is seen in the Levens Hall pieces. It is possible, as some have suggested, that pieced quilts were a comparatively late invention, and that they could have been independently developed in the New World. I feel it is more likely that it was a known style of work when the settlers came to America, and that they brought examples or the knowledge of it with them.

The development of pieced-style quilts had been stimulated by the arrival of the gay, easy-to-sew, washable, and color-fast Indian chintzes. It was these, and the domestic cottons from the industry they inspired, in conjunction with the inventive spur of necessity, which began that new development and direction in pieced quilts which was to come to such remarkable fruition in America.

3 The Colonial Period

More than a century before the ladies of Levens Hall made their pieced bed furnishings, the first English settlers had arrived in the New World. These settlers, and others who followed, quickly established living patterns based on their various backgrounds, the conditions they had left, and those they found themselves in when they arrived. Differences in cultural inheritance, social philosophy, religion, aspirations were, naturally enough, expressed in the institutions they created, the ways of life they formed, the things they wanted and made.

Although the long sea miles separated the colonists physically from their homelands, they carried with them the taste that had been formed there and in many cases the actual objects extracted from the old environment. The settlements were originally planned and financed by entrepreneurs who were members of the establishment, under charters granted by their rulers. And while some may have wished to leave behind everything of the Old World, more rested content during the long colonial period with the close political, emotional, and aesthetic ties which bound them to Europe, ties which, especially in the English colonies, were continually renewed. Governors came and went, trade was extensive, wealthy colonists sent their children to England to be educated or themselves went—some to stay, some to return. Europe was the original source of taste, and while regional differences can be seen among early crafts, they had in common their European derivation; their models were remembered forms and things transported to the New World.

It is quite certain that quilts were among the household furnishings given precious space on the first small ships to the New World. Travelers had to provide for themselves on those long voyages, and quilts, or featherbeds, those stuffed bags which had served time out of mind as both mattress and cover, were an obvious solution to hard bunks in chill holds. And it is likely there were some fine quilts carefully tucked into chests with other treasured household items.[1]

In addition to those bedcovers which arrived with the settlers, importers, from an early date and continuing for a long period, and in answer to what must have been a considerable demand, brought in a large variety of quilts. Mr. Adam Leyland offered in the Boston *News-Letter* for March 21-28, 1723, among eight-

Figure 12. Appliqué quilt, patchwork border. America, c. 1850. Cotton. 76″ x 69″. An example of the overall symmetrical appliqué design-type not done in the block-style. In motifs drawn from nature, as in the eagles, appliqué quiltmakers often stylized their subject, extracting and accentuating the essential forms. (George Schoellkopf)

een varieties of materials, ". . . Bed-Camblets, Cotton Quilts, and Deck Nails."[2] The Boston *Globe* for May 27, 1746, advertised "English Goods, a great variety imported from London, in the last ships"; and among the cloth, notions, apparel, and hardware were "bed Quiltts."[3] That same paper for October 5, 1761, had "a few English made Carpets, some very large Bed Quiltts . . ." for sale by Lewis de Blois.[4] And this from the Boston *News-Letter,* May 13, 1762: "Imported from London, and sold by Moses Belcher Bass, . . . Quarter Blankets, Quarter Bed Quilts, Quarter Coverlids. . . ."[5] It would seem from the advertisements that many of these were of English manufacture, made for home consumption and export.[6]

From such early newspaper accounts and advertisements we have at least a faint picture of the kinds of quilts and covers in use among the more comfortably situated colonists in that period: common featherbeds, quilts both English and Indian, some of the cotton variety, and some bedcovers, which may or may not have been quilted, of rich materials, silks and damasks, some embroidered in the English manner, and those which might have been made here no doubt much in those styles then in fashion in Europe, styles of which the colonists were keenly aware. As early as 1675 preachers in controlled New England were railing against the apeing of London fashions. A century later, a visiting Englishman, W. Eddis, "saw very little difference in the manner of a wealthy colonist and a wealthy Briton."[7] What, then, can we say with any certainty about the types of quilts the colonists were making for themselves? Unfortunately, we are again hampered by a lack of evidence, for nothing of the early period survives. But it seems certain by inference that they were making quilts; a little quilted clothing has come down to us, and there are other hints, such as this advertisement in the Boston *News-Letter,* June 22-29, 1727: "Quilts, Rugs and Wadings . . ." the last almost certainly for quilted articles. In the same paper, August 20-27, 1716, "George Brownell, late school Master in Hanover St., Boston" offered to teach "Quilting."[8]

It is my feeling—and I label it thus—that the first American quilts were most likely plain quilts made of sturdy whole cloth brought by the first settlers or imported soon after they arrived and that among these first quilts were some of a technically pieced variety made by joining random sizes of scraps together, most likely trimmed into squares or rectangles because such shapes are the easiest to work with; given the normal predilection for symmetry, such quilts might even have had some regular pattern (a woman faced with a large piece of blue material and several smaller strips of brown might put a brown strip on each side, framing the blue, rather than simply joining them haphazardly).[9] Some evidence for this survives in early linsey-woolsey quilts—some are of whole cloth; others, showing the marks of salvage, are in arranged stripes or blocks,

Figure 13. Patchwork and appliqué marriage quilt, Maine, dated 1785. 86" x 81". The earliest dated American quilt I know of which employs pieced work. An inscription reads: "Anna Tuels her bed quilt given to her by her mother in the year Au 23 1785." In some areas of the country, hearts signify a bridal quilt; elsewhere, they may have been simply tokens of love. (Wadsworth Atheneum)

Figure 14 (right). Patchwork and appliqué quilt. New England, c. 1793. This central-medallion-style quilt is one of the few dated eighteenth-century American quilts with pieced work. In the borders can be seen patterns—Wild Goose Chase and Variable Star —which are still made. (Winterthur Museum)

often of contrasting colors, indicating they were put together from the remnants of worn-out whole-cloth quilts.

It is not until the last quarter of the eighteenth century, however, that we have any irrefutably American quilts to look at. In the collection of the Wadsworth Atheneum there is what is to my knowledge the earliest dated American quilt showing pieced work (figure 13). It is inscribed "Anna Tuels her quilt given to her by her mother in the year Au 23 1785," and has a wide, plain, and elaborately quilted wool border, then multiple inner borders in the Yankee Puzzle pattern surrounding a central square, with its center a segmented circle. The bulk of the inner work is pieced, with some appliqué. The eight hearts it shows may mean it was a wedding quilt, for it was the custom in some areas to decorate quilts destined for the nuptial bed in that way. In the collection at Winterthur there is a pieced and appliqué quilt made by Mary Johnston (figure 14), who initialed and dated it in 1793, and combines fine appliqué figures cut from English fabrics arranged around a central tree motif, with an outer Wild Goose Chase border. An undated quilt in the collection at Mount Vernon is reputed to have been made by Martha Washington (figure 15); it is, in any case, from the last quarter of the eighteenth century and American. It has a piece of copper-plate printed chintz in the center depicting William Penn's treaty with the Indians, a European material of a pattern known to have been sold in Philadelphia in 1788.[10] Surrounding it are eight borders: one floral appliqué; the rest, pieced geometric motifs in

Figure 15. Patchwork quilt, Pinwheel. Virginia, c. 1785. 100¾" x 100". According to tradition, this quilt was made by Martha Washington. Its center is a piece of an English copper-plate printed cotton with a scene called "Penn's Treaty with the Indians," a material which was known to have been for sale in Philadelphia in 1788. It is pure central-medallion style, with appliqué and pieced elements, indistinguishable from similar English quilts of its time, and typical of such examples from the end of the eighteenth century. (Courtesy of The Mount Vernon Ladies' Association)

patterns still popular. It, too, has a Wild Goose Chase border, and in the corners, the same Variable Star blocks that appear in Mary Johnston's quilt. All three of these are practically indistinguishable from English quilts of the same period, which often had pictorial center squares around which were arranged successive borders of appliqué or pieced designs, a mode largely abandoned in America after the eighteenth century but continued in England until the present day. This central-medallion style, usually with borders and decorated corners, very possibly developed from the popular Indian palampores, a number of which, made for the Western market, had that general format (which had itself been influenced by Western design): a rectangle with a central motif often echoed in corner designs, and surrounded by single or multiple borders.

These three quilts illustrate America's ties to England based both on cultural affinities and economics. They are made predominantly of English materials. England's colonial policy had been directed toward the protection of her own industries and the preservation of her outer possessions as a source of raw materials and a market for her finished products. She had from the beginning attempted to discourage an American textile industry; the colonists had been equally concerned with insuring themselves a supply of domestically produced fabrics. In 1640 the General Courts of both Massachusetts and Connecticut decreed that every family plant and raise a certain amount of flax. By 1644 there were 4,000 sheep in New England, and ten years later the General Court of Massachusetts decreed that ewes might not be exported. The next year they were busily engaged in determining how many members of each household in their domain could give how much time to spinning, and quotas of spun yarn, with penalties for non-performance, were levied against each family. In the last years of the seventeenth century, England, alarmed at increasing colonial production of woolen goods, outlawed not only the export of finished cloth but its trade from colony to colony. The spinners and weavers, however, continued their work. To judge from existing records, the home production of textiles was a busy occupation.[11]

But England guarded well the secrets and machinery of her sophisticated textile industry. In addition to wools, linens, and silks, they were sending fine English-made cottons, since as early as 1676, English manufacturers had mastered the secrets of mordant dyeing and were block-printing their own color-fast cottons; soon these were coming in quantities to America. So while the colonists made much cloth for home consumption and even sale, their industry was limited in scope and geared to the production of practical fabrics, linens and wool "homespuns." For more sophisticated and finer materials for clothing and furnishings, they relied on imports. Indian chintzes came in the seventeenth century and were as cherished here as they were in Europe.[12] Florence Montgomery, in her book entitled *Printed Textiles,* gives these import figures for fabrics: 1756, 90,616 yards; 1785, 353,762 yards; 1800, 3,710,471 yards, a rather astounding increase, pointing up the lack of effective American competition.[13]

The beginnings of America's cotton textile industry were at Pawtucket, Rhode Island, where in 1790 Samuel Slater reproduced—from memorized plans—Arkwright's English textile machinery. But it was many years before American cottons could compete with the British. America continued to export her raw cotton to England to be converted into textiles. In 1791, two years before the invention of the cotton gin, which facilitated the processing of raw stock, America exported under two hundred pounds of raw cotton. In 1793, it was 487,000 pounds; in 1800, 20,000,000.[14] English textiles prevailed by force of superior technology and a long-established marketing system which gave American merchants liberal trade terms on English purchases, often deferring payment for long periods.[15] Even after the War of 1812, ". . . England flooded the United States with cheap cottons, in many cases sold at a loss in order to sell and to discourage the American industry."[16]

So materials available for quilts were largely a combination of American homespuns and English manufactures; this explains the great variety and quantity of English materials which appear in American quilts until after mid-nineteenth century; and the usual placement of such materials—homespuns for the back, English printed fabrics for the top which would be seen—is indicative of American taste of the time.

The central-medallion style of the three late eighteenth-century quilts discussed, so similar in appearance to English quilts of the same period, illustrates the strong European—and particularly English—influences on fashionable colonial taste. Colonists eagerly followed European vogues, and had from the beginnings of settlement. The Revolution, while it forever altered America's political relationships with Europe, did little to change fashionable taste. ''Political independence did not radically alter America's reliance upon England either for manufactures or for cultural guidance. Men like Noah Webster called for a brand-new start toward a purely American way of life. '[Americans] must believe, and act from belief, that it is dishonorable to waste life in mimicking the follies of other nations and basking in the sunshine of foreign glory.' '' [17] But taste and fashion, were not, after all, what the Revolution had been about. It was those things in the realms of politics and economic affairs which caused the break, not dresses and furniture.

This is not to say that the things made in the colonies were exact copies of foreign models, for there were subtle forces at work which would bring about an ''American'' look in New World products. Among the many reasons for the changes which did occur in the design of fashionable furnishings were the availability and variety of materials, differing environmental and social demands, the level of expertise of emigrant workers. There was in general a simplification of imported forms, in some objects toward a more ''sculptural'' statement, less

Figure 16 (above, left). Pieced linsey-woolsey. Pennsylvania, c. 1785. 86″ x 76½″.
A schematic rendering of the central-medallion style, in two colors, indicating the center piece, multiple borders, decorated corners. This is the high-style in a utility quilt, all the details eliminated for quick and easy working. This pattern persisted as a block, as in figure 17. (Courtesy Mr. and Mrs. Foster McCarl, Jr.)

Figure 17 (above). Double Square. Pennsylvania, c. 1870. 83½″ x 75″. The double-square block, a single one of which formed the early linsey-woolsey quilt in figure 16, is used here in a repeated manner almost a century later.

detailed embellishment, and often more open surfaces. The "American" look which developed in high-style furnishings can be clearly seen in furniture and other decorative arts in the many documented examples which have survived.

America's distinctive pieced quilt tradition, however, had its origin in covers made more for utility than show. The earliest surviving examples of such quilts are what have been called "linsey-woolsey" quilts. Found in our northeastern states, they date, at least those which have survived, from the latter part of the eighteenth into the early part of the nineteenth century, after which they seem to have passed from vogue. Thus they were made during the same period, and in the same areas, as the bordered central-medallion-style quilts we have discussed; I would think it possible that both kinds could have been made in the same family. Linsey-woolsey is a sturdy material of linen or cotton warp and wool weft (other materials which are not true linsey-woolsey are often included in the category); quilts made with it used a filler of wool, the whole obviously designed for hard use in a cold climate. The majority of those found are made of whole cloth in solid colors, usually a different color front and back. Often the top is of linsey-woolsey, probably imported, and the back of a coarser homespun material. The colors range from indigo to madder to delicious sherbert colors. Their beauty, aside from the appealing texture and colors of the material, comes from the fine quilting patterns in which they were sewn, swirls of feathers, hearts, flowers, baskets of fruit. Rarer ones, however, and those which are of interest to us, are made up of what appear to be pieces of other worn-out linsey-woolsey quilts or garments. Figure 18 shows such a pieced linsey-woolsey quilt of the latter part of the eighteenth century; it retains the English central-medallion style, but is composed of scraps of thirteen different colors, trimmed into rectangles for ease in assembly,[18] the whole a kind of "drawing" of the style, its intricacies reduced to a broad format.

These linsey-woolsey quilts are the earliest examples we have discovered of the pure block-style quilt in America, and indicate that this was a style originally developed for the making of utility, rather than "best," quilts. The quilt in figure 16, dating around 1785, is a schematic of the central-medallion style, its complexities (multiple borders, textures, patterns, designs, and colors) skillfully reduced to a two-color format which emphasizes the broad strokes of the design rather than the preciousness of the individual materials from which it was made. What is particularly interesting about this quilt is that the overall design will be adapted for a pieced block—figure 17 shows a quilt using this identical block, also made in Pennsylvania, but fully a hundred years after the linsey-woolsey. These two illustrations show how a single block can be used as a motif for an entire quilt, or in a repeating manner in the more conventional fashion.[19]

Figure 18. Central-medallion style. Massachusetts, c. 1790. Linsey-woolsey. 93″ x 74″. Scraps of thirteen different linsey-woolseys have been used to piece together a primitive but unmistakable bordered central-medallion-style quilt.

The linsey-woolsey quilt in plate 10, dates around 1790 and shows that Wild Goose Chase border seen in the Mount Vernon quilt (figure 15) extracted and used as a design motif. Yet the "sense" of the English quilt—borders surrounding a center—is still there. The way in which a single motif, normally reserved for a border design of a more elegant quilt, has been developed into the overall pattern for an entire surface, is interesting and American. This is not truly a block-style design, but shows how, using only immediately available scraps, the simplest design idea, and color variations, a utility quilt of strong visual impact might be quickly made. It also shows how the visually elaborate, often busy, format of the central panel quilt can be reduced to a serene design scheme. In the fourth example, in plate 11, dated around 1800, the Variable Star motif (seen in the corners of the two inner borders of the Mount Vernon quilt, figure 15—and another pattern still used today) has been blown up and used as an overall design; this block-style quilt has a distinctly American look. The final example, plate 12, from around 1790, has been cut to fit a four-poster bed; it goes even further in the American direction—a combination of strong colors and simple forms has produced an aggressive, yet harmonious, design.

The source of such quilts was in the tradition of functional design. This tradition developed in a particularly American way from its basis in the store of practical knowledge brought by her first settlers. I will follow this into the nineteenth century, when the American pieced quilt comes into its own as a design form.

Plate 1. Cat appliqué. New York, c. 1850. Cotton. 88″ x 84″. A superb appliqué quilt, demonstrating the graphic possibilities of the technique. Common Pennsylvania "folk" images—hearts, tulips, birds—have been interpreted and combined in an extremely free manner to create a striking overall composition. The birds look a bit like penguins, the pine trees have hearts at their tops, one kind of flower grows from another—and the cats with the calico eyes sit watch. (America Hurrah Antiques, N.Y.C.)

Plate 2. Princess Feather appliqué. Pennsylvania, c. 1880. Cotton. 86″ x 84″. Princess Feather is one of the most popular appliqué and quilting patterns. This is an unusually exuberant and bold design in the strongest colors, but not altogether surprising considering its Pennsylvania background. (Collection of David and Susan Cunningham)

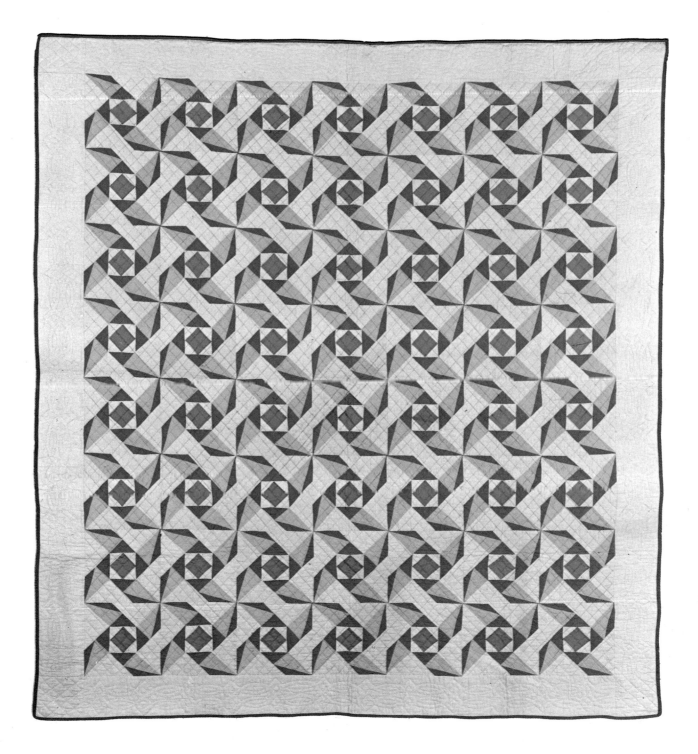

Plate 3. Eccentric Star. Pennsylvania, c. 1910. Cotton. 87½″ x 81″. Through the use
of subdued and contrasting colors and design elements, this quilt achieves an
unusual quality which suggests twisted, flattened ribbon.

Plate 4 (left).   Section of Indian chintz made into a quilt. Coromandel Coast, first half of eighteenth century. Cotton. A detail of a typical piece of painted Indian cotton—a chintz. This was not originally a quilt; borders of silk (not shown) and a linen back were added, and the whole quilted after the fabric arrived in Europe. (Cooper-Hewitt Museum of Design, Smithsonian Institution. Accession No.: Textile 1968-79-1)

Plate 5 (above).   Mariner's Compass. New Hampshire, c. 1820. Cotton chintz. 96″ x 96″. This popular Eastern coastal pattern was taken from the card of a ship's compass. Pieced from English chintzes, it shows the beautiful, soft pre-aniline dye colors of those materials. (Collection of Kelter-Malcé)

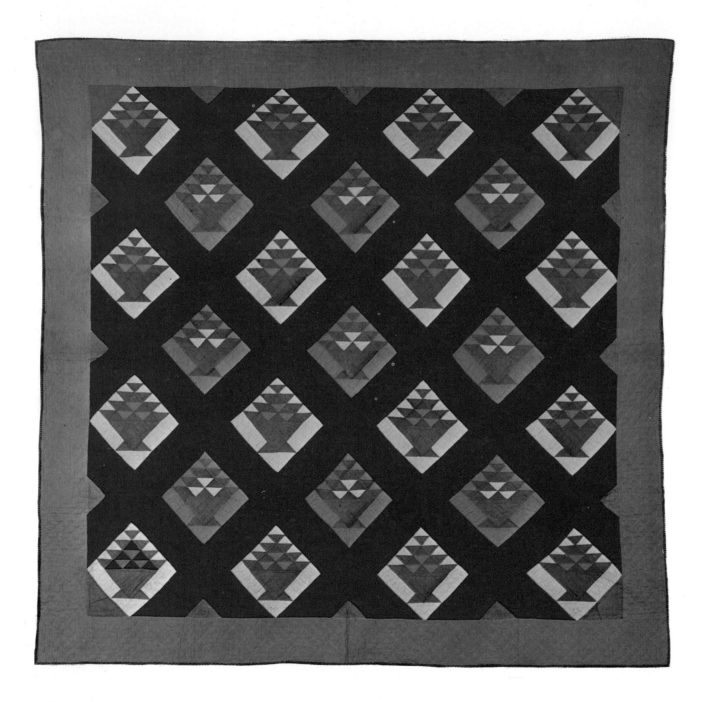

Plate 6. Basket or Flower Pot. Pennsylvania, c. 1880. Cotton. 74″ x 72″. The singularly different block in the lower left-hand corner was done in white either because the maker had run out of yellow or because she did not wish to make a perfect quilt; some thought such perfection was an affront to God, and many quilts show deliberate imperfections.

Plate 7. Wild Goose Chase—Stars. Pennsylvania, c. 1890. Cotton. 86″ x 86″. Glowing
red against a recessive blue-green, this quilt has the aura of a mystical drawing.
(Collection of Bill Gallick and Tony Ellis)

Plate 8. Star of Bethlehem. Newburgh, New York, c. 1815. Cotton chintz. 120″ x 120″.
Such big Star of Bethlehem quilts were commonly made in both England and the
United States from the last part of the eighteenth century through the early nineteenth
century, undoubtedly as ''show'' quilts. For this American example, the maker
reserved her pieces of the fine English chintzes. (America Hurrah Antiques, N.Y.C.)

Plate 9. Rainbow or Joseph's Coat. Pennsylvania, c. 1890. Cotton. 84″ x 71″. The diagonals seem to push the central block of vertical stripes forward, giving the feeling of order emerging from the swirl of creation. It is a brilliant transcription of a natural phenomenon to abstract design.

Plate 10. Wild Goose Chase. Pennsylvania, c. 1785. Linsey-woolsey. 90" x 90". This particular pattern usually has both pieced and appliqué elements, but here is rendered completely in a single pieced design motif. This quilt is notched on one end to fit the posts of a four-poster bed. (Privately owned)

Plate 11. Variable Star. New York or Pennsylvania, c. 1800. Glazed linsey-woolsey.
93¼″ x 77½″. Pure block-style in the late eighteenth or early nineteenth century; the
sherbert pink is typical of linsey-woolsey colors. The Variable Star is one of the oldest
pieced quilt patterns. (Courtesy of Mr. and Mrs. Foster McCarl, Jr.)

Plate 12. Cross. New York, c. 1790. Linsey-woolsey. 98½″ x 93½″. A fine American statement in color and form, the block-style here moving toward a more sophisticated and intricate statement. Such distinct separation of the blocks with solid materials between was the early form. (Courtesy of Mr. and Mrs. Foster McCarl, Jr.)

Plate 13. Geometric Star. Pennsylvania, c. 1885. 83″ x 83″. Here the overall star motif has been forced into a more right-angled format. The interplay of the muted colors is brilliantly orchestrated. (Collection of Blanche Greenstein and Tom Woodard)

4 The Nineteenth Century and Functional Design

Functional design has always existed side-by-side with the products of fashionable taste, and can be seen in "folk" objects and tools the world over, and of all ages. At first, having some general notion of the age of many pieced quilts I saw, I was struck by their "modern" look in general and their visual similarities to products of some of the painting movements of the last several decades in particular. As I began to establish firmer dates for these quilts, I was impressed by how anachronistic the images seemed for the eras in which they were made. For example, many of these clean and simple geometric patterns were made during the heights of Victorian embellishment; their colors, bold and bright or subtly modulated, are in sharp contrast to the painting and furnishing colors and effects of their period.

Plate 14 is one half of a stereoscope card, used in the simple three-dimensional viewing device first made in mid-nineteenth century. The card dates near the end of the nineteenth century, and is a typical subject popular with home viewers of that era. Four little girls seem to have just awakened; they are in a brass bed, and the furnishings of the room are those elaborate copies of Classical and Renaissance materials jumbled together in the fashionable manner of the period. On the bed, however, is a finely worked red and blue quilt; the pattern is Flower Baskets with a modified Sawtooth border—the whole, simple and elegant. If it were extracted from its setting and hung on a plain wall, it would have the same "modern" feeling of so many quilts of that period.[1]

It is obvious that there were two traditions or movements at work, producing objects of widely disparate styles which were used concurrently.[2] This phenomenon has been well analyzed in an important study of functional design, *Nineteenth Century Modern* by Herwin Schaefer, published in 1970. Schaefer wrote:

In the nineteenth century, functional form existed in the technical realm. . . . It existed in the field of transportation, in carriages, ships, trains, in sports equipment and in musical instruments. And it existed in the vernacular: the design of age-old everyday useful objects whose forms were the result, over centuries, of intuitive adaptation to function, originally on the basis of traditional hand-craft

Plate 14. Stereoscope Card, c. 1895. Image size: 3″ x 3″. The contrast between the vernacular design tradition and "high-style" decoration is vividly demonstrated in the unadorned geometry and simple colors of the handmade Basket quilt seen with machine-made copies of early fabrics.

*production and, in the nineteenth century, more and more of industrial produc-
tion. While artistic ornateness was the mark of the ruling taste, the vernacular
flourished on a more modest level in all areas of the home furnishings field. It
produced the unassuming and undecorated functional form in furniture, glass,
pottery, and other household equipment as a matter of course. The common
concern of technical and vernacular design was function. In both realms,
throughout the nineteenth century, designs were produced that are "modern"
in the sense that they strike us as apt and contemporaneous today, even though
made long ago. In this sense "modern" is not necessarily synonymous with
machine design; it rather denotes an approach to design, the direct, practical,
and best solution of a problem, regardless of technique. Nor does "modern" in
this sense refer to artistic or stylistic peculiarities of a period—though that period
be the modern period—but to the timeless qualities derived from the logic of
function.*[3]

The process of the creation of vernacular designs, always fueled by necessity, was one that had begun with the first settlers and had continued as the country expanded in the nineteenth century, opening new lands to settlement with new problems to resolve. The pioneer-settler, in a way perhaps difficult now to envision, was on his own. Solutions to the problems he faced often could not be found in previous experience, but, rather, through an open approach to the situation from which would come the appropriate new tools and methods.[4] These tended to be the simplest and most expedient possible—for he had no labor or materials to spare. This will be reflected in architecture, tools and household furnishings, and work systems as well as political and social institutions. There was an attitude toward design which emphasized functionalism "without any blind adherence to old established forms or precedents," one which shaped both the everyday objects of the house and the products of technology.

The block-style pieced quilt was an example of this functional approach to design, its roots in an earlier time, coming to full flower in the nineteenth century as a new form. The pieced quilt was a "utility" quilt (in contrast to the appliqué quilt which was a "best" or show quilt, upon which much time was lavished) and though there were some elaborate examples made which took every bit as long as the most involved appliqué quilt, it was in general the everyday bedcover, and designed to be made quickly. The block-style was the result of a functional approach to the solution of a problem. Bedcovers had to be made, and in quantity. Money was scarce, and whole cloth expensive. So from otherwise useless scraps of cloth salvaged from clothesmaking and worn-out cloth articles, the American woman pieced together a useable piece of fabric which became

Plate 15. Baskets. Pennsylvania, dated 1902. Signed "L.F.G." Cotton. 78" x 76". I consider this a masterwork. It is composed of highly geometricized flower baskets, linked and arranged so that their elements form a large and harmonious abstract surface. The interplay between small and large design elements and the two colors gives the surface much movement, but just enough so that the pattern is not shattered. It is the essence of the tradition. (America Hurrah Antiques, N.Y.C.)

one side of a quilt. The block-style pieced technique in which pieces are cut into largely geometric, straight-edged forms was itself the most efficient method, in terms of both time and material, for using surplus fabric and joining it together. (Backs were often pieced also.)

The block-style pieced quilt could have had a separate evolution, its earlier forms now lost; blocks do show up in late eighteenth-century high-fashion quilts of mixed pieced and appliqué techniques (figures 14 and 15). Or it could have evolved from one of the overall geometric quilts in the Levens Hall style. We have mentioned the Levens Hall hangings and quilt (figure 10), the earliest manifestation (1708) so far discovered on either shore of a repeated geometric motif approach to a quilt top. The overall design of these pieces, using many repeated figures arranged in a regular sequence, was not constructed in block fashion; that is, the quilt was not made of blocks worked separately to be complete designs within themselves and then joined together, but rather the pieces seem to have been joined together progressively. This style survives in a number of quilt patterns still made, such as the Star of Bethlehem and Baby Blocks, examples of which are included in the plates. Such quilts can be constructed in block fashion (but not in the square-block style favored by Americans): a popular early geometric pattern in this style was the Beehive or hexagonal patch quilt, in which hundreds or thousands of perfectly cut hexagons were pieced one to the next until the finished quilt took the shape of an overall honeycomb pattern (plate 85). This quilt can be made either by building pieces on one at a time, or by working in blocks (segments formed by starting with one hexagon in the center and building pieces around it in ever-larger circles until a desired size is obtained). These blocks can be of a regular pattern if the same color scheme is followed for the pieces in each one; they can then be joined together and will interlock perfectly, with hexagons added where needed. This development would be a natural one where it was desired to obtain an ordered effect using different colors and textures of materials. Precious as the materials might have been, quiltmakers preferred to trim them into geometric shapes rather than piece them as they came as in the crazy quilt which might use all of the material but would not have given the ordered end result they desired. And in general such progressive piecing is a more time-consuming style of work than piecing blocks of the same pattern to be later joined together; many of the shapes are bias-cut, which requires very exacting sewing to fit the seams correctly, and in the case of such patterns as those using hexagonal pieces, the shapes must be sewn over paper templates which are later removed. The earlier quilts of this type usually are superbly made of fine material, and show all the marks of being the proud products of households where necessity was not the master.

Figure 19. Kaleidoscope. Pennsylvania, c. 1869. Cotton. 70½″ x 73″. A quilt pattern that exploits optical possibilities. See plate 16 for detail.

The block-style method of quiltmaking is a time-saving device in which individual, identical blocks can be pieced one by one and later joined together. It is also space-saving, not a minor consideration given the cramped quarters of much early American rural living. (G. Francis Dow mentions that in seventeenth-century New England a house eighteen by twenty-four feet could house seven or eight people.[5]) Though larger homes followed as the colonies prospered, those who went to the frontier repeated the "huts and hovels" of early New England. The cabins they built were crowded with implements, children, bedding, cooking utensils, a few pieces of furniture, drying food, and the like. Blocks could be "lap-worked" one by one in contrast to the cumbersomeness of a progressively larger and larger fabric as would be the case if a quilt were made in the Levens Hall manner.[6]

The block-style can be divided into two categories: quilts in which the blocks can each stand alone in terms of the design, and quilts in which the blocks have been joined together as integral parts of the overall design. In the former, exemplified in such quilts as plates 17 and 18, the overall design is a combination of isolated blocks which repeat the same pattern and their accompanying borders and separating strips, often called "sashes." In the latter, while the individual blocks have a separate identity, the overall pattern is formed by the manner in which the parts of the blocks interact when they are joined. The first category is self-evident. The second is further divided into those overall patterns formed by symmetrical blocks, those formed by asymmetrical blocks, and those formed by blocks which are split, usually into two equal triangles (each half may be composed of smaller pieces of materials in squares, rectangles, or triangles), one half of light-colored material and the other of dark.

The first quilt type, constructed from symmetrical blocks, is evident in the Kaleidoscope pattern (figure 19). As can be seen, each block is composed of eight triangles, alternately of dark and light materials, their apexes meeting in the center, with four added triangles of light material in the corners to make a square block (see block marked out on detail photograph, plate 16). Individually, each block gives the sense of a circle within the square; when joined together, the light and dark parts match up to form larger light circles enclosing four-pointed stars with circular "pinwheel" centers. As with many quilts of this type, there are other subtle and complicated forms produced, which the eye will

Figure 20 (below, left). An individual Sailboat block, one of the asymmetrical types, is outlined. The entire surface is built from that block alone. Such asymmetrical blocks can form many different overall patterns depending upon how they are used in relation to each other. One result is the quilt shown in figure 21.

Figure 21 (below, right). New York, c. 1880. 74" x 60". A quilt formed by using only the Sailboat block. Such startling possibilities were fully exploited by quiltmakers. (Rhea Goodman, Quilt Gallery, Inc.)

Figure 22 (above, left). Nine-Patch variation. Pennsylvania, c. 1935. Cotton. Here the blocks are positioned to form the Barn Raising pattern, the same overall design which is often seen in Log Cabin quilts, which are similarly composed of half-light, half-dark blocks.

Figure 23 (above, right). Nine-Patch variation. New Jersey, c. 1945. Cotton. The blocks are arranged to form an unusual overall pattern.

suddenly pick up so that the whole surface pattern changes, in much the same manner as "optical illusion" drawings can be seen first one way, then another. Such exploitation of the optical possibilities of patterns was quite intentional.

The second type, an asymmetrical block called Sailboat, is perhaps even more startling in its final result. The block (figure 20), sketched in on the detail, is pieced of one large and five small white triangles, one dark triangle, a large and a small trapezoid. (The complete quilt is shown in figure 21.) Completely different overall patterns could be made with the same blocks simply by altering the way they are positioned in relation to each other. In the case of either symmetrical or asymmetrical blocks, it is extremely difficult to envision what the overall results will be from the contemplation of a single block. As can be seen, square symmetrical blocks which are meant to be linked will always form the same pattern no matter how they are turned in relation to each other. Asymmetrical blocks can be used to give many different overall results by varying their orientation within the format.

The third type of linked block is illustrated in color plate 19 and figures 22 and 23. Typically, a square is divided into two halves diagonally to form two equal triangles, and the block is composed of squares or rectangles of material. In one half of the block, materials light in color will be used, and in the other, dark. This is the basis of the famous Log Cabin block, a number of examples of which can be found in the plates. In plate 19, the block is a Nine-Patch variation, one of the simplest in the quiltmaker's repertoire, formed, as the name implies, from nine equal-sized squares. (The possible variations on this seemingly simple scheme are enormous.) To find the block, simply look in any corner of any of the three quilts (plates 19 and figures 22 and 23) and count three rows by three rows, and that is the basic square block, many of which would have been made to form the quilt. On each side of the light and dark division there are three full square patches and three triangles either all in dark or all in light materials. The method of construction was this: the maker pieced a number of squares of material divided just as the overall block is, half of light and half of dark material. These were all then assembled as can be seen in the block, with the divided squares put into the center, their dark halves forming with the dark patches, their light with the light. As many squares of this type as were needed for the overall dimension of the quilt were pieced, and then they were joined. What is immediately evident is that, by a simple variation on the way the light and dark segments of the finished blocks were positioned, three totally different results were obtained. The overall quilt pattern in the color plate is called Straight Furrow because of its resemblance to the paths of a plowed field. (Normally, a quilt takes its name from the name of its block, if the block can be used only one way—as in Kaleidoscope. If the block can be used to form different overall patterns, the quilt is called by the block name with a second overall design name, as in a Log Cabin—Barn Raising quilt.) Figure 22 is Barn Raising, so called, I believe, because of its resemblance to the laid-out segments of a barn section, assembled on the ground before erection. The third quilt's proper name I do not know, and perhaps there is none (figure 23). The quilt shown in plate 19 deserves careful scrutiny because in it can be seen the extraordinarily sophisticated effects quiltmakers achieved with the simplest of means. A close study of the fabrics will show that many of the textiles used in the dark sides of the blocks appear in the light, but that none of the very lights, white, yellow, pink, or light blue, appear in the dark. The eye then reads the strong, regular dark stripes and overlooks the inconsistencies in the light. In the second example, figure 22, there are light materials in the dark, and dark in the light. The majority on each side, however, are of the proper intensity; the eye will then compensate for the irregularities, and the effect of the dark and light pattern will be maintained. The effect is an extremely subtle one; in the Straight Furrow example it looks as if strips of smoked glass had been laid over the body of an evenly colored quilt, changing the tonality of what is underneath, when in fact it was simply a skillful manipulation of those tonal differences in the materials available to the maker of the quilt which created the effect.

There is another pieced quilt type which is not dependent on blocks, yet is assembled from components, and that is the strip quilt and its variants, as can be seen in plate 20, Stripes, and plate 21, the Rainbow quilt. In the latter, the strips forming the "teeth" are pieced of alternating light and dark triangles, then sewn to the solid strips. (In the north of England, which shared some pieced quilt patterns with the United States, such quilts were called "strippies.")

The question is asked, who figured out these complicated patterns? It has often been said that many of them came from ladies' magazines of the nineteenth century, particularly *Godey's Lady's Book,* a magazine for the middle class and those aspiring to it.[7] But a reading of its entire run from its inception in 1830 to its last issue in 1898 revealed only some seventy-five patterns for pieced work; of these, fewer than five were designed in block-style, the rest were to be made of small components each pieced to the next in the ancient manner exemplified in the Levens Hall quilt. (And many of the rest of the designs they

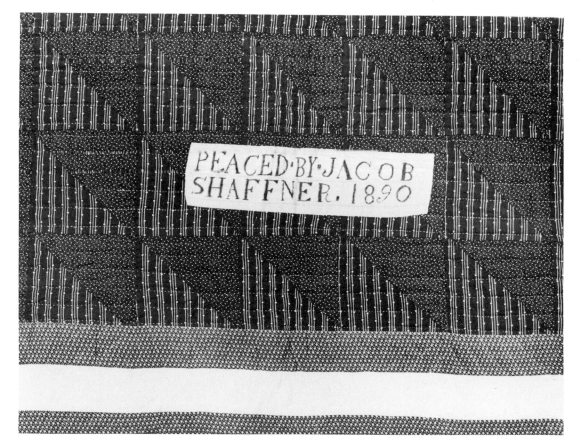

Figure 24. Little Sawtooth. Pennsylvania, c. 1890. Jacob Shaffner, proud of his work, added his name to the quilt he made, much as professional Pennsylvania weavers signed their coverlets. Quilts which can be attributed definitely to male workmanship are extremely rare. (America Hurrah Antiques, N.Y.C.)

offered had obviously not been designed by anyone who had successfully done pieced work.) *Godey's,* it seems, was catering more to the later nineteenth-century craze for silk pieced work, performed as a genteel pastime, than to those who made quilts of cotton and wool to keep their families warm. Other magazines of the period, designed more for the rural audience, make little or no mention of quilts and carry no patterns—an indication that for those readers, it was no more necessary to discuss how to make pieced quilts than it would have been to describe how to fill a pail with water. The women who made functional quilts—and made up the patterns—were largely unschooled, and certainly not trained in geometry. Yet they, and perhaps their husbands, had a practical knowledge of design which they used in their daily work.

Masculine hands are not so often evident in quilts, though they are occasionally there. The illustration, figure 24, shows a detail from a Pennsylvania quilt proudly signed "Jacob Shaffner," who "peaced" it in 1890, much as he might have signed his axe handle or any other implement he made. (Plate 21 shows a Rainbow quilt with a stenciled ownership mark, most likely done with the same stencil Mr. Reitz used on his wagons and other possessions; he probably did not make the quilt.) There are records of men doing patchwork, both here and in England. American folk commentary discloses that a betrothed young man would often design a quilt for his fiancée to make as part of her trousseau for their new home. And I have found a few indications that some quilt patterns may have been designed by country farmer-builders for their wives; their practical knowledge of geometry would have been of much use in such an endeavor. However, it is my feeling that the great majority of these patterns were designed by women who exploited the possibilities of simple divisions and arrangements of the square.

Blocks were commonly made in this manner: a known pattern was chosen, or a new one invented. It was of course important to get the maximum use out of each piece of material, so the square was studied to see how best it could be divided to avoid waste. The pieces had to be cut accurately; pieced patterns rely upon the most exact cutting of their parts; otherwise, the blocks will not go together correctly, or their parts will not line up properly if they are to be set with other blocks, or the whole quilt will be out of square, creating considerable problems when it comes time to put it in the frame for quilting. If the pattern was based upon the simple divisions of the square, and most were, templates, to insure accurate cutting, would be made by folding paper of the proper size to form the parts. Cuts were made along these folds and the resulting forms used either as they were as cutting guides or as patterns to make templates from a stiffer material, cardboard or metal (the latter sometimes cut by obliging hus-

Figure 25. Reverse Appliqué. Pennsylvania, c. 1880. 86″ x 86″. An unusual appliqué quilt, based on the paper cut-out work practiced with great dexterity in Pennsylvania. Hearts, tulips, birds, typical motifs are evident. (Collection of David and Susan Cunningham)

Figure 26. Gothic Windows. Pennsylvania, c. 1890. Wool. 71″ x 69″. Based on a pattern derived from the Gothic motifs which were repopularized in the nineteenth century, this quilt indicates the ability of the geometric-based block-style to encompass varied design forms.

bands). This method could be used even for designs which might appear to be very complicated. In patterns which included circular parts, the formal basis was still the square, with arcs or circles cut out following patterns drawn with a compass or some simple circular object, a teacup or small plate, available in the home. We have reproduced the diagram and instructions for an overall pattern called Arabic Lattice, from Ruby Short McKim's *One Hundred and One Patchwork Patterns*.[8] It is typical of the kind of cuttings which are involved in any of the intricate patterns based on the square. Once the pieces are cut, they are sorted by shapes and colors, and drawn on as the blocks are assembled, much as one would in assembling a standardized part. The important thing in this scheme, as I have mentioned, is that the block must always be square, the pieces cut precisely to size and sewn accurately; then all parts will mesh when the blocks are assembled. This was, in effect, a system of interchangeable parts—the basis, in the industrial sphere, of America's great technological growth in the nineteenth century.

There were a number of sources for designs. Some were, as we have seen, simply geometric figures which can be found in other places and times and in other mediums. Such designs as Baby Blocks, Nine-Patch Block and its many variations, and the many star patterns, such as Star of Le Moyne ("Lemon Star"

in the vernacular) and Variable Star, can be found in Roman and Arabic mosaic floors and architectural decoration, Renaissance decorative inlay, marquetry on furniture, and the like, their sustained popularity due to the convenience of working with divisions of the square in techniques which require piecing together parts of contrasting colors. They do not necessarily descend from a common source, but would be reinvented by people who set about to work with the square as a basic block for a pieced technique.

Some designs were direct visual abstractions of objects and natural images: Ocean Waves, Wild Goose Chase (the triangles represented the wedges of geese which passed with the seasons), Mariner's Compass (the card of a nautical compass), Sawtooth. A smaller number were visual representations of ideas: Drunkard's Path (twisted, difficult to negotiate, meandering), Burgoyne Surrounded (the red English infantry square encircled by files of small squares, the American irregulars). There were direct images: Coffee Cups, Schoolhouse. And there were the many appliqué patterns of forms taken directly from nature. Rarer were those drawn from such sources as the cut-paper work practiced in Pennsylvania, usually for valentines (figure 25, an appliqué quilt). Architecture lent some motifs: figure 26 shows a pieced pattern, Gothic Windows, drawn from

Figure 27 (above, left). Nine-Patch variation. Pennsylvania, c. 1820. 94″ x 94″. Made from chintzes and figured cottons of the 1820s, the quilt is in block-style but retains a vestige of the central-medallion-style quilt with the chintz pheasant and four roses carefully arranged at dead center. The pieced blocks with figured materials between are typical of block-style quilts of this era.

Figure 28 (above, right). Birds in the Air. New England, c. 1820. Chintz. 89″ x 80″. An early block-style quilt, the design elements spread over the surface in a fashion which characterized American pieced quilts. The pattern is an ancient one, one of a number of variations of a similar motif, very popular in early America.

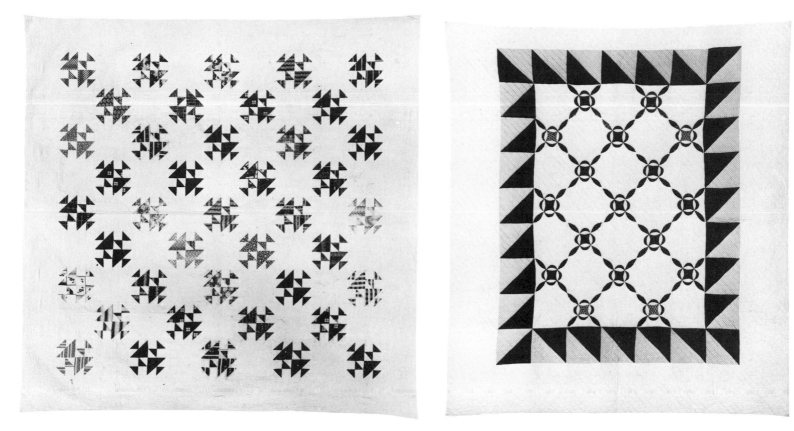

Figure 29 (above, left). Old Maid's Puzzle. New Jersey, c. 1805. Chintz. 97" x 97". The block-style in an early manifestation, the pattern opening up in a manner which was to become typical of many American quilts.

Figure 30 (above, right). Reel; Sawtooth border. Pennsylvania, c. 1850. 94½" x 84". A bold, thoroughly American statement. The center pattern, the ancient Reel, is made of chintzes from the 1830s; the aggressive border is done in printed materials from perhaps ten years later. The conjunction of delicate rounded forms and the angularity of the border have been well planned for a striking effect.

Gothic-style decoration; the Courthouse Steps pattern shows the frieze, columns, and steps of a Greek-Revival building; and of course, there is the Log Cabin pattern.[9]

Most designs were given names meaningful to the makers and drawn from the whole realm of the American experience; nature: North Carolina Lily, Bear's Paw, Pineapple, Fly Foot, Spider's Web; religion: Delectable Mountains (from Bunyan's *Pilgrim's Progress*), Tree Everlasting, Forbidden Fruit, Jacob's Ladder, World Without End, Star of Bethlehem, Job's Tears; politics: Whig's Defeat, Kansas Troubles, Lincoln's Platform, Jackson Star; historical movements and events: Nelson's Victory, Free Trade Patch, Rocky Road to Kansas, Underground Railway, Kentucky Crossroads; games: Johnny-Round-the-Corner, Leap Frog, Puss-in-the-Corner; places: Philadelphia Pavement, New York Beauty, Indiana Puzzle; common objects: Monkey Wrench, Fan, Indian Hatchet, Hour Glass. These marvelous titles, so expressive of American sensibilities (Yankee Pride, Fifty-Four-Forty-or-Fight, True Lover's Knot), could be extended through the hundreds of pattern names indicative of the fervent quiltmaking which went on for over three centuries.

There was in the nineteenth century a continuing evolution of quilt design toward an increasingly distinct American expression; I illustrate four quilts, which used mostly English chintzes and calicos. The first, figure 27, from about 1830, while in the block-style, retains, almost as an afterthought, the central medallion —in this case, a pheasant cut from an earlier chintz; between the nine-patch blocks are squares of a floral chintz. The overall feeling is one of complexity and busyness for the sake of "elegance." The next, figure 28, made about ten years later, uses a Birds-in-the-Air asymmetrical block in rows of an alternating "up and down" sequence; while the pattern is still a bit involved, the interspaces have been done in white, which opens up the design somewhat. The next, figure 29, made about 1845, uses an Old Maid's Puzzle block, the motif set boldly on a white background. In the fourth, figure 30, which dates from around 1850, sections of the Reel pattern, done in chintzes, are centered on a plain background and surrounded with a bold Sawtooth border, the whole framed within white. The chintz colors are madders, browns, deep greens; the Sawtooth is strong red and yellow. The overall effect is bold and individualistic, with a sharp contrast between the delicate tracery and colors of the chintz Reel pattern and the aggressive Sawtooth border of small-figured calicos.

The inventive furor of the nineteenth century, which rapidly changed many established methods of making things, brought important innovations in the textile industry. Experiments in chemical dyes, begun early in the century, brought new colors to the textile spectrum. At the same time, new methods in textile technology, such as roller printing, vastly increased machine production of fabrics. In 1840, an estimate of hand versus machine printing of fabrics in Great Britain per day was 168 yards as against 5,600 to 14,000 yards.[10] This new technology meant the eventual end of hand-printing of fabrics on a commercial basis. While England continued to export cottons to the United States, the American cotton industry had come into its own. Now there was a tremendous variety of cottons available, in bright new colors and patterns. American women had more raw material to experiment with; what had once been so precious was now widely available, and they responded with a fury of quiltmaking which continued almost into the twentieth century. In terms of design, it was the most important period, since after a long evolution, a distinctly American style had been achieved, and its possibilities were thoroughly explored during more than half a century.[11]

The materials themselves often have a subtle effect on quilt design. The strong and large-scale design elements in floral and pictorial chintzes often suggested certain arrangements. It is common to see quilts in which particular fabric patterns have been used to create or strengthen visual effects; often a bold stripe or curve will be set against a fine figure, a dot or small flower, creating contrasting patterns within the overall design. Of course, this is an extremely subtle process, practiced with greater and lesser effect depending on the visual skills of the quiltmaker. But certainly it was a factor which entered into each woman's determinations as she sorted her materials and considered the "look" she wished to achieve.

The invention of aniline dyes shortly after mid-century meant the appearance of some vibrant new hues—mauves, alizarin red, then greens and browns, some more successful than others. (The chemical composition of some of the early brown dyes caused it eventually to corrode the cotton, which accounts for the many quilts of mid-century which show holes wherever there was brown in the pattern.) The subtle red tones of madder dyes were replaced by the strong aniline reds, and American women employed them lavishly in their designs. They were used extensively in conjunction with the new greens (which have not aged well) shortly after mid-century, at first to make what were evidently considered elegant appliqué quilts; no doubt their novelty commended them, just as had that of the chintzes more than a century earlier. As they became more common, they were used equally lavishly in pieced quilt designs, the reds sometimes employed to make common patterns in that color only, on a white background, a style which lasted well into the twentieth century.

As the nineteenth century progressed, machine production of copies of once-expensive handcrafts swelled enormously, in answer to popular demand. Siegfried Giedion wrote in *Mechanization Takes Command:* "Men born in the first quarter of the nineteenth century grew up in the belief that all products embodied labor values and were to be won only by long toil. But now the machines began cutting to a fraction of their former cost not only cotton goods, but almost every product used in art and adornment."[12] The copies did not retain the simplicity of many of their models, but were elaborated often beyond recognition. It was a taste fostered among all classes. Renaissance-style curtains and hangings, Oriental-style rugs, Greek-style vases, Gothic-style furniture, though in much adulterated form, became widely available. Architecture took in every style known since Hellenistic civilization, with emphasis on the most elaborate, curvilinear, and romantic. Americans had become "culture" conscious, and this meant filling their homes with copies of largely European cultural artifacts. At the same time, the traditions of functional design continued in rural areas and among people who rejected, could not afford, or had no access to the products of the over-blooming high style—"ruling taste," as Giedion calls it.

The difference is perhaps best shown by comparing two quilts; the one in plate 22 is dated 1887 in the quilting; the other one, shown in plate 23, is dated 1883 in embroidery. The first exhibits what are to me many of the best qualities of the functional approach to quilt design we have been discussing: it is a utility quilt, made in response to a need; it was quickly made, of large pieces sewn by machine, in an unusual crystal-shaped block (each block has one yellow square and one each of a red and blue diamond); the red and blue segments were easily obtained by simple cuttings of a square; the design is a skillful manipulation of simple geometric forms, the square and diamond, for sophisticated visual effects; the design is open and clear; the colors are bold, and the whole thing can go into the wash. The second is made from silks and velvets in the late nineteenth-century style of "genteel" work. While constructed as a quilt, it was made for display; the corners are fans, the rest of the blocks are pieced in the crazy quilt style. (It is perhaps appropriate here to say that I am certain that that term, about which there has been some confusion, means "crazed" in the sense of fractured, the first definition given in Webster's Unabridged for "crazy": "full of cracks or flaws"; that is, having the appearance of crazed pottery, broken into irregular segments. While some may seem to be the work of lunatics—I know of one which has embroidered on a simple black velvet patch, in the midst of the most incredible profusion of textures, colors, embroidered animals, plants, and countless "show" stitches, "I wonder if I am dead"—I think the derivation I have stated is the correct one.) It is encumbered with elaborate embroidered flowers, animals, initials, insignias (some in dimensional, raised work), and in all ways is typical of that style of silk and velvet patchwork which was a fashionable craze near the end of the nineteenth century. The design is cluttered, incoherent; the point was to use as many different colors and textures of rich materials as possible, in as many shapes, and to add an embroiderer's textbook of different stitches and effects, all for "enrichment" and "elegance." Typical of such work, there seems to have been little thought spent on the overall design; it is a near-sighted view of minute, sectional effect, as in an illumination, rather than the longer-range view of total effect, as in a painting. It was not meant for practical use; the work is fragile, as are the materials; it is difficult to clean. It is practically useless as a cover and impossible as design, and it took hundreds of hours to make. A judgment which Herwin Schaefer applied to the eighteenth century is equally apt here; he saw "a 'two track' production—the one utilitarian, functional, matter-of-fact, the other a matter of prestige, of aesthetic, and social differentiation. . . ."[13]

The production of these ornamental quilts began before mid-century. The first reference we find to piecework in *Godey's* (which we must remember was addressed more to city women and the middle class than rural subscribers) is in the issue of January 1835. It shows a hexagonal Beehive pattern in that style which had been popular in England since the eighteenth century. *Godey's* saw patchwork as a fine way to use up leisure time. From the January 1857, issue:

As the time of year is fast approaching for those happy in-door evenings with their pleasant and easy occupations which help to make home so dear, we think it requisite that we should offer a suggestion for one of those tasteful works which are of ceaseless variety in their execution, and are, when completed, worthy of becoming family heirlooms.[14]

From its beginnings as an ornamental pursuit, silk patchwork grew, by the last quarter of the century, into a craze.[15] The ideal in these quilts was that which existed for all of the fashionable art of the Victorian era: the rejection of simplicity and the right angles of unadorned geometric form. A *Godey's* article in May 1883, "Mosaic Patchwork," says:

It saves time if a few of the smaller pieces are joined by a sewing machine, but we would suggest only a little of this being done, as it gives straight lines. If, on completion, there are any angularities offending the eye, they can be hidden by the application of ovals or other curved forms of silk being put on the top and worked around.[16]

And, speaking of the fantastic variety of stitches with which crazy quilts were embellished, the April 1883, issue says: "The greater the diversity in stitches the better. . . ."[17] It had ceased, for these women, to be a functional craft. From the November 1851, issue: "As a change from the accustomed routine of knitting, netting or crochet, the production of ornamental patchwork will be found an agreeable occupation."[18] Its status as a genteel occupation was unquestionably established.

This was not the case, however, for all American women. Quite the contrary. The functional tradition was not submerged by Victorian "high" taste; necessity still ruled in the country. As late as 1883, an article entitled "Bed Clothes" in *Arthur's Home Magazine* began: "Three-fourths of the bed covering of our people consists of what are miscalled 'comfortables;' viz: two calico cloths, with glazed cotton wadding laid between, and quilted in."[19] Earl Robacker speaks with authority in his *Touch of the Dutchland,* a book on Pennsylvania folk art published in 1965, of days "with the temperature at ten below zero and small snowdrifts forming on the window sill because of an ill-fitting sash, five [quilts] were none too many, as the writer knows from experience."[20] Most American women, out of necessity, continued to make the clean-lined and simply patterned pieced quilts in the block-style they manipulated with such dexterity. *Demorest's Monthly Magazine* for August 1867, offered "patterns for patchwork, from which our country readers may select designs, not intricate yet very effective . . ." a tacit recognition of the simpler designs traditionally favored by those living away from centers of fashion.[21]

Not that rural families escaped the blight of Victorian decoration. In *The Good Old Days,* a volume of reminiscences of American country living, it was said that an "all silk quilt in intricate design set a woman high in the community," one would guess as much from the display of this expensive material as from any intrinsic design merit in the quilt.[22] It was an intrusion of materials unsuited to rural use, and an elaborate design that was fashionable but not functionally derived. No doubt the same woman who made a fancywork quilt for the parlor was also making simple geometric pieced quilts for her family's beds, the former a manifestation of "ruling taste" with its forms characteristically submerged in embellishment, the latter grounded in the ageless tradition of functional design. It is the latter which are truly an American manifestation of timeless design principles. When the American woman wished to apply her better sensibilities, she could transmute even the excesses of ruling taste to simple beauty. The crazy quilt format, with unnecessary decoration removed and organization applied, could produce such quilts as that in plate 25, organized in blocks, each of which has a central focus of red which tends to draw the design together. Others of the type commend themselves by their bold organization of colors and form, such as that of plate 26, signed by the Nicely sisters, Eva and Susan. It is those crazy quilts which were planned largely as a surface on which to display embellishment that now seem decadent to us.

When the extraordinary nineteenth century ended, American women were still making both the labored products which descended from Victorian high taste and the simpler but visually more sophisticated quilts which had emerged from the vernacular tradition. The former continued to be made for several decades, and are in retrospect not really quilts at all (few were actually quilted, as this would have interfered with the surface work, and usually were tufted instead); they were not functional. When the reaction against Victorian sensibilities inevitably occurred, those quilts went the way of most other decadent design of the era. The block-style quilt continued.

Plate 16. Kaleidoscope detail. A single block, of the symmetrical type, is outlined on the detail, showing how larger patterns of the quilt are formed by the linking of the parts of adjacent blocks. The complete quilt is shown in figure 19.

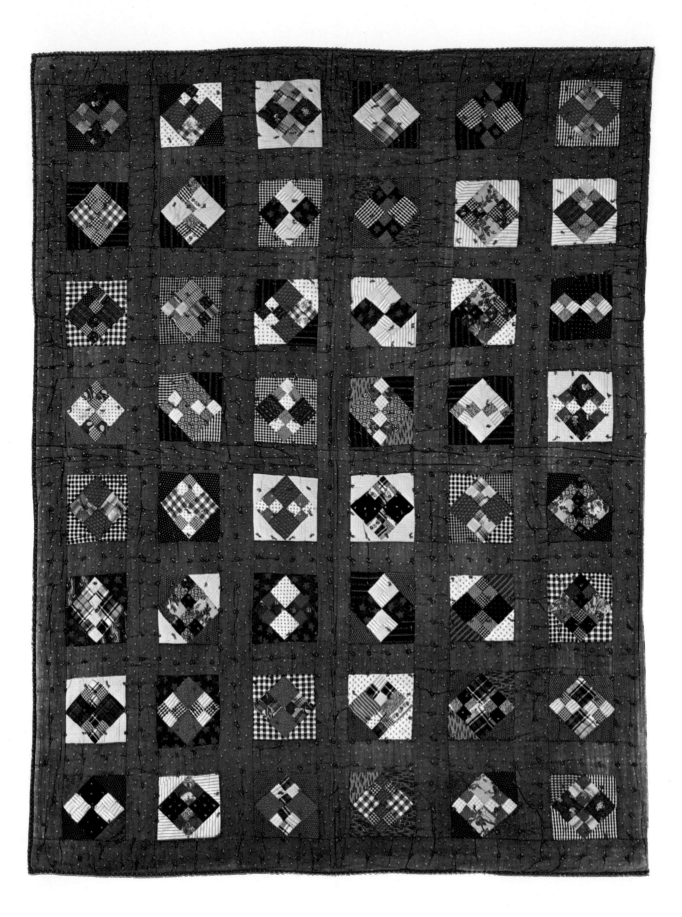

Plate 17 (left). Improved Four-Patch. Pennsylvania, c. 1860. Cotton. 86" x 65". This quilt evokes for me both glimpses of other galaxies and the abstract beauty and movement of electronic circuitry.

Plate 18 (above). Variable Star. Pennsylvania, c. 1855. Cotton. 87" x 87". One of the earliest quilt patterns, enlivened by Pennsylvania color sensibilities—spots of pinks, greens, yellows, and blues on a surface which is held together in a yellow grid and pinned down with red squares.

Plate 19. Nine-Patch—Straight Furrow. Pennsylvania, c. 1875. Cotton. 75″ x 73″. A variation of one of the simplest patterns. Count three rows by three rows in any corner to find a block; the same block can be used to form a number of different overall patterns.

Plate 20. Stripes. Pennsylvania, c. 1880. Cotton. 84″ x 84″. One of the simplest pieced quilts to run up, just strips of material which can be quickly sewn by hand or machine. Pennsylvania quiltmakers were expert at balancing the colors and proportions of such quilts.

Plate 21. Rainbow. Pennsylvania, c. 1880. Cotton. 80″ x 73″. In an unusual gesture, the owner of these quilts, E. S. Reitz, stenciled his name in the lower left corner, much as he would have marked his other prized possessions.

Plate 22. Broken Star, Carpenter's Wheel, or Dutch Rose. Pennsylvania, dated 1887.
Cotton. 82″ x 79½″. Contrast this quilt, dated 1887 in the quilting, with plate 23. Made
during the same era, it demonstrates the concurrent existence of two design trends,
one springing from a functional tradition, the other concerned with fashionable
embellishment.

Plate 23. Crazy. Pennsylvania, dated 1883. Signed ''L.'' Silk and velvet. 69'' x 67''.
Victorian fancy needlework all but submerges this quilt, dated 1883, even though it is
organized in blocks. The attention to minute detail assumed more importance than
overall design harmony.

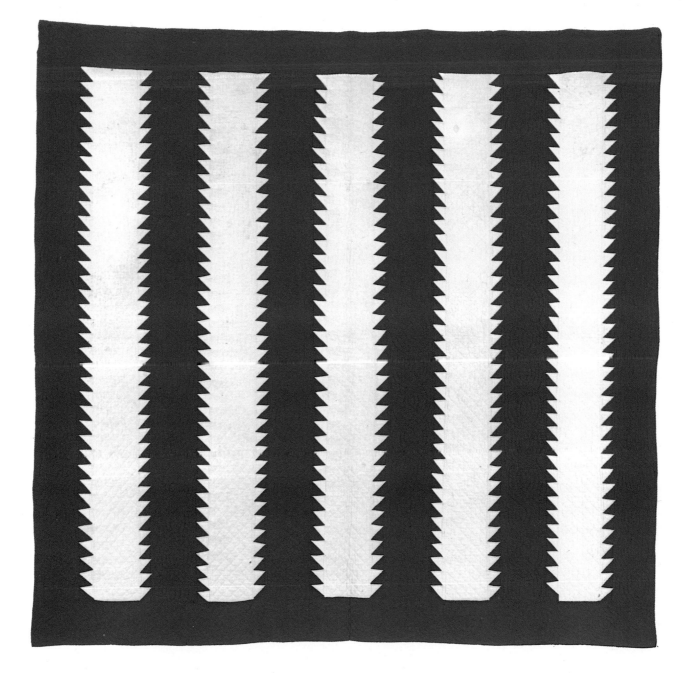

Plate 24. Tree Everlasting, Path of Thorns, Herringbone, Arrowhead, or the Prickly Path. Pennsylvania, c. 1850. Cotton. 73″ x 72″. Simple but always effective, this old design has many names. But the first name—Tree Everlasting—reflects the early American's intense involvement with his religion.

Plate 25. Crazy. Pennsylvania, c. 1865. Wool. 88″ x 70″. Here, the often unruly crazy format was organized into blocks, and the blocks were built around a central red focus. Quilts of this type often look like aerial landscapes.

Plate 26. Crazy. Indiana, c. 1890. Silk and velvet. 72″ x 70″. The Nicely sisters, M. Eva and Susan, made this mostly from dress silks, laying on ribbons in the center in a fine expressionistic manner. The surrounding crazy blocks are unusual for their large and bold sections, but entirely in keeping with the aggressive design sensibilities of the Nicely girls.

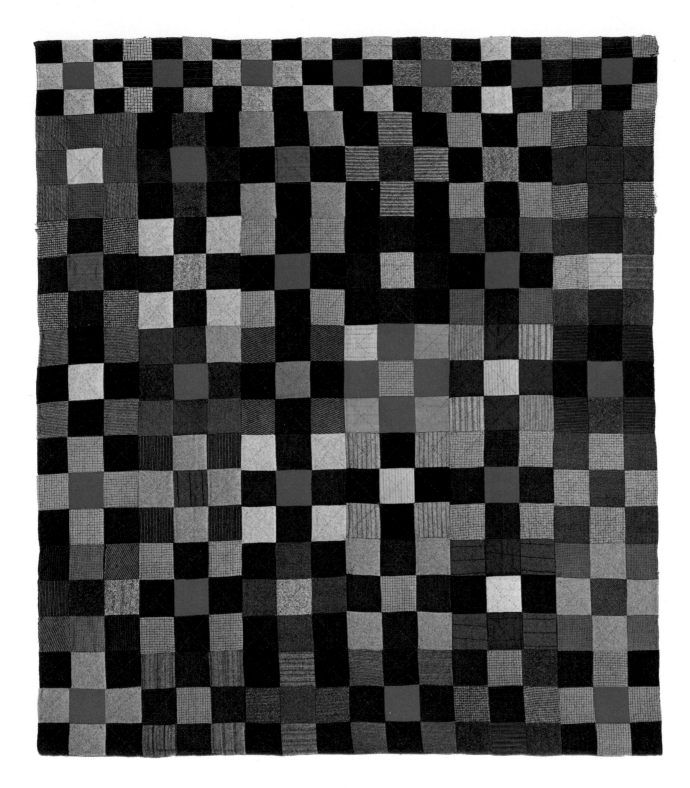

Plate 27. Hired hand's quilt. New Jersey, c. 1890. Wool. 74″ x 64″. The essence of the functional approach, a hired hand's quilt made in the simplest manner possible from squares of men's suit materials. Atypically, the maker could not resist adding just enough patches of red to turn a dull surface into a meaningful design.

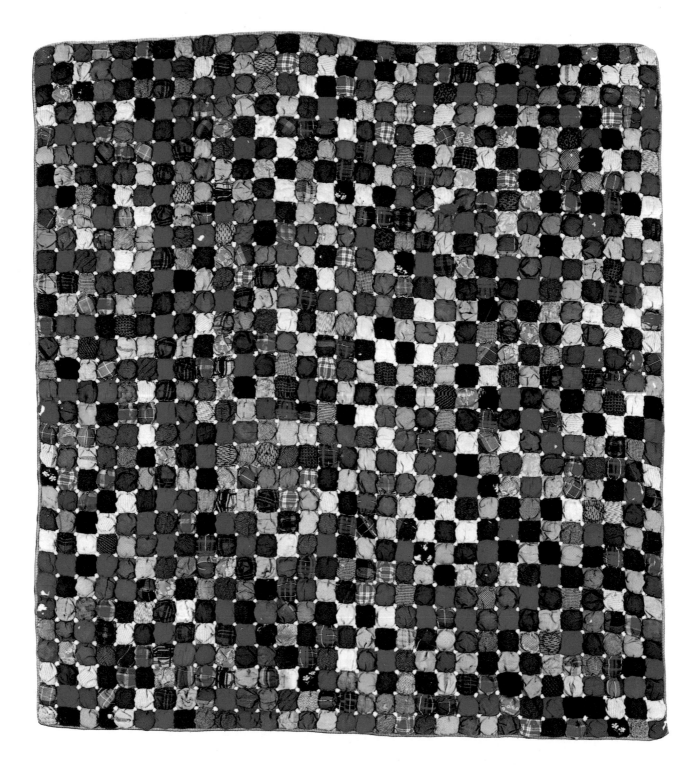

Plate 28. Puffs. Maine, c. 1875. Wool. 76″ x 70″. Most stuffed work is in fancy quilting, but here the whole quilt is composed of half-spheres of padded-out material. The result is quite playful and must have been a rather startling note on a bed.

Plate 29. Thousand Pyramids or Triangles. Pennsylvania, c. 1870. Cotton. 80½″ x 78″.
Reminiscent of Cubist-derived abstractions, there is a continual visual interplay of
triangular forms building up and down into larger and smaller overall triangular
patterns.

Plate 30. Rocky Road to Kansas. Pennsylvania, c. 1865. Cotton. 86″ x 68″. The green diamonds in the design can link visually to make large stars, which seem to be set within circles—an example of the visual complexity quiltmakers achieved with simple means.

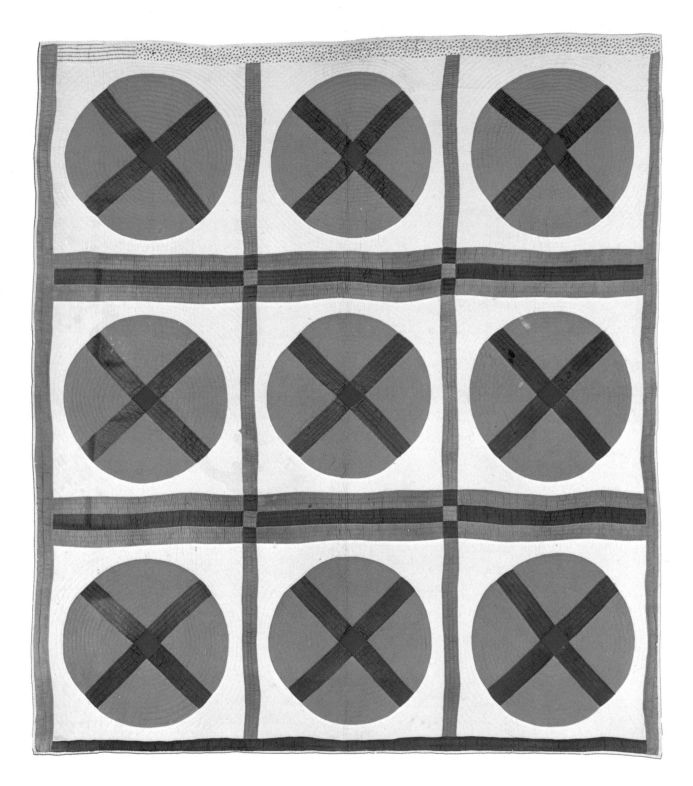

5 The Quiltmaking Scene

Although it might seem that a great many American quilts have survived the advent of inexpensive machine-made covers, central heating, and electric blankets, the remaining quilts are but a small fraction of the total that were made. To my knowledge all the quilts from the seventeenth century have vanished. Almost all of the much greater number from the eighteenth century are gone; those quilts that we do have left are largely of nineteenth-century origin, and most of them are from mid-century on. It is difficult to estimate how many were made originally. The claim in *Arthur's Home Magazine,* mentioned before, that in 1883 three-quarters of American bedcovers were quilts, indicates the continuing need for and use of quilts in the American home through the nineteenth century; at that time the country's population was still over 80 percent rural, and the economy and milieu which encouraged the making of pieced quilts still prevailed. In rural Pennsylvania, for example, "Necessity demanded that the construction of bedding take primary place, and the fabrication of it was accepted by everyone as a household task, an inevitable part of every woman's life. Into its contriving went all spare moments and all the scraps of cloth saved from the making of garments."[1] It is probably safe to say that in earlier times almost all American homes used some quilts, along with their home-woven blankets, if they were not, by force of circumstance, using skins to cover their beds. It is equally probable that for a very long period almost all American women made quilts.

In many parts of the country there was a custom that a young girl make a baker's dozen of quilt tops before she became engaged, twelve utility quilts, undoubtedly pieced, and one great quilt, pieced or appliqué, for her bridal bed. After her engagement, she would take final steps to turn her tops into finished quilts, and these went with her as an essential part of her trousseau. It was the beginning of a life of quiltmaking. Writing in 1849 in *Godey's,* T. S. Arthur, in a story, "The Quilting Party," said: "Our young ladies of the present generation know little of the mysteries of 'Irish Chain,' 'Rising Star,' 'block work,' or 'Job's Troubles,' and would be as likely to mistake a set of quilting frames for clothes poles as for anything else. It was different in our younger days. Half a dozen handsome patchwork quilts were as indispensable then as a marriage portion; quite as much so as a piano or guitar is at present. And the quilting party was

Plate 31. Circles and Crosses—unique pattern. Colorado, c. 1900. Cotton. 84½" x 75". A unique design enhanced by quilting which follows the circular forms; such continuously curved quilting is quite laborious in comparison to straight-line sewing. (Collection of Philip and Gail Holstein, Aspen.)

equally indicative of the coming-out and being 'in the market' as the fashionable gatherings of the times that be."[2]

In an account of several incidents in the Ozarks related to quilts, Kathryne Travis spoke of going to a log cabin and being shown quilts which belonged to the inhabitant, an old woman: " 'Yes'm, I got a right smart o' quilts, but I don't know as you'd think they's pretty.' We were climbing the short flight of narrow, enclosed stairs to the attic room of the log cabin. 'You see, me and the girls have a right smart o' time after we get the crops laid by, so we usually have a quilt in the frame. I managed to give all my four sons and three married daughters enough quilts to keep 'em warm, and now these here [drawing back a muslin curtain and displaying a stack of neatly folded quilts higher than my head] these here, belong to Emmie and Pearl. Leastways they will as soon as they git them a man. I don't want any o' my chillern sayin' I ain't done right be 'em by not givin' 'em plenty of good warm beddin'.' "[3] This same custom—of providing children with quilts at their weddings—is still practiced by the Amish of Pennsylvania. "All mothers by tradition make a few quilts and comforters for each child. These are usually made years in advance so they will be ready when needed. One housewife made three quilts and two comforters for each child; she had seven boys and three girls."[4] (A "comforter" is a thickly-padded cover usually smaller than a quilt and usually tufted through rather than quilted.)

In most households where quilts were made and used, and that means most households, the majority were simply used up. Recounting another of her experiences in the Ozarks, Kathryne Travis tells of seeing a Drunkard's Path quilt hanging on a clothesline; she stopped to talk to the owner.

A row of heads could be seen at the edge of the door, a hound began to bark, two small children ran behind the smokehouse and peered from their hiding place. "Hello," I called. A tall, gangling woman came slowly forward in the light. Behind her, clinging and hiding, were four small, dirty, ragged children. "May I get a drink of water here?" I asked. "Yes, I reckon so. Hey, you, Hennery, run down yander to the spring and tote up a bucket of fresh water fur the lade." Henry emerged from behind the smokehouse, and keeping his eye on me, he picked up a lard bucket and slowly vanished. "That's a bright quilt you have on the line," I said. "Did you make it?" "No'am, my old man's ma made hit. The chillern's been usin' hit fur a pallet here on the porch, and out in the field to put the baby on." Three chickens wandered out of the house and jumped off the porch. "Hit rained last night and everything got wet; I jes' hung it out to dry." I looked through the door; the floor was half gone and the roof full of holes.

"Have you any more quilts as pretty as that?" I asked. "No, we useter a lot, but they's all been used up. My old man's ma was a hand at makin' quilts. She

made one with over six thousand pieces in hit, but the young uns done tore hit up." I then saw an ironing board leaning against the wall. It was covered with the remains of a quilt scorched and browned almost beyond recognition; it was the "Tree of Paradise" design. I managed to find a complete block visible, in which I counted one hundred sixty-five pieces. I later estimated the quilt to contain twenty blocks, making four thousand one hundred and twenty-five pieces in the quilt. . . ." [5]

While she criticizes, in the end, the "shiftlessness" which would prompt such careless destruction of such beautiful objects, this was no doubt, in less drama-tized versions, the fate of the vast majority of American pieced quilts, even if they were carefully used. Quilts, like all things made for utility, served their pur-pose and were discarded.

Any kind of projection of how many might have been made is subject to the widest speculation; it certainly runs into the millions, so the number left actually seems tragically small. A good many did, however, survive from the later nine-teenth century, the period during which I think the most interesting and impor-tant design contributions were made. So while we mourn the loss of what must have been a multitude of superb quilts, we must consider it fortunate that many have survived from a great period.

That survival was due in part to the large number made during a time when they were increasingly less necessary. In better-built, larger, and warmer homes, and with the arrival of machine-made covers, what quilts were made were used less, and were less subject to the hurly-burly and hard wear of crowded, basic living conditions. Many were not used at all, and were carefully, with respect for the labor which had gone into them, put away.

Thrift was dear to the hearts of Americans, and quiltmaking was a salvage art. Nothing was wasted if there was an ounce of good left in it.[6] Speaking of the colonial woman and her attitude toward fabric, Frances Lichten recounts: "Al-ways conscious of its cost, the housewife made use of even the tiniest fragment. An examination of any early piece of home needlework will show how general was this regard for fabric. During recent generations, the piecing and patchwork of fragments has been considered a sign of thriftiness in which there was more than a tinge of miserliness, but the colonial housewife, limited to her scanty supply of fabrics and quite honestly concerned about it, frankly used bits of material often no larger than an inch in diameter, to eke out a section of a gar-ment or a quilt patch in order that it could be made entire and therefore useful."[7]

Women spent a life-long servitude to needle and thread in the centuries pre-ceding the present, and still do in areas of the world where manufactured prod-ucts have not supplanted home industry. They were apprenticed to that exacting master at an early age; in the United States, well into the nineteenth century, little girls as young as three were taught to sew. One method was to give them a scrap of material and have them count a certain number of the woven threads, putting in a stitch every so many threads. Soon they could sew a straight line with almost machine-like regularity. A major part of the curriculum of girls' schools in the eighteenth and nineteenth centuries was sewing.[8]

The introduction of the sewing machine in mid-nineteenth century somewhat altered the ancient dependence on hand-sewing. There was evidently a simple machine on the market in France as early as 1848. Elias Howe in the United States had a finished model in 1846, and others soon followed. *Godey's,* February 1854, in an article entitled "The New Sewing Machine," took its first notice of the invention, noting that "It is so *simple* in its construction and action that it may be worked by a *child,* and will sew a circle, curve, or turn a square corner, equally as well as a straight line."[9] By 1855 it was saying: "These valuable aids to female industry are becoming quite a familiar thing in private families. . . ."[10] In one year in the 1870s, 600,000 sewing machines were sold.[11]

Godey's, September 1860, saw the sewing machine's use in quiltmaking: "In quilting, and all kinds of stitching, they seem indispensable. . . ."[12] A separate home quilting attachment for the sewing machine was actually invented by a Henry Davis of Chicago, and appeared in the *Scientific American* for March 18, 1892. With it one could quilt "comforts, quilts, coat linings, dress skirts, and any other article which it is desired to have filled with cotton or wool."[13] It used a roller system which handled top, back, and filler in conjunction with the sewing machine. Such devices were, it seems, little used, for quilts with machine-run quilting are a rarity. But machines were extensively employed in piecing quilt tops; about half of all quilts we have seen which date from the 1860s on are machine pieced. Some appliqué quilts are also machine worked, but they are the exception. The sewing machine was commonly used in both types, even if the quilts were otherwise completely worked by hand, for finishing edges, a boring job. Pride in handwork kept some women from using machines in their piecing. Also, the handwork which went into a quilt was evidently a form of relaxation, a relief from the drudgery and real labor of family maintenance in frontier and rural America. It was the woman's outlet, often her only one, for her feelings for form, color, and line. Quilts were often the only spots of color in a drab rural home, a visible proof of the feminine arts of the household. Special quilts were carefully tucked away, to be put on the bed of an important visitor. Their successful construction was a mark for young girls of their fitness for matrimony. It was a chance for each woman to invent her own designs and pit her skills against those of her neighbor, in a society in which such skills were among a woman's chief outward signs of worth.

In her recounting of Ozark customs, Daisy Stockwell mentions the picnics to which men would bring their finest livestock, women their best quilts and other handwork, and samples of their choicest recipes. While the men vyed in athletic contests, the women hung their quilts on lines strung between the trees.[14] Quilts were judged with other valued home products at those regional fairs which flourished all over the United States in the nineteenth century. Frances Lichten mentions that the Lehigh County Agricultural Society's first fair in 1852 "offered a premium of $1.00 for the best quilt, $.50 for the second best," while "Miss Hewsom of Coopersburg, 'whose elegant quilt made of 14,000 pieces,' received only an honorable mention. . . ."[15] It is encouraging to note that sheer amount of work in a quilt was evidently not the only criterion for judgment. Quilts were prized, not only for fine workmanship, but also for their beauty, the associations particular patterns had for people of a region, their subtle but daring innovations on familiar themes, and the visible expression they were of culturally valued feminine virtues of thrift, industry, application, care of the home.

Fairs and other communal gatherings were responsible for the transmission of quilt designs. An unusually interesting new pattern, the invention of a particular woman, or popular in a particular region, would be seen, duly noted, and carried away by women to their homes, and to different regions. It has been said that a new design would be held in memory and the block pieced when the seamstress was back in her house to be stored as a "sketch" for future reproduction. Migration, of course, also took designs from one region of the country to another; a family going West, or brides going to new homes, took their quilts with them, where their patterns would be seen by new neighbors. Some designs can be traced from their origins on the Eastern seaboard into the West; the Ship's Wheel of Maine became the Harvest Sun of the prairies.[16] Ruth Finley mentions one pattern which acquired, with its changing locales, some fourteen names: Indian Trail, Forest Path, Winding Walk, Rambling Road, Climbing Rose, Old Maid's Ramble, Storm at Sea, Flying Dutchman, North Wind, Weather Vane, Tangled Trees, Prickly Pear, and Irish Puzzle.[17] Some women kept pattern collections of favorite blocks, and no doubt exchanged patterns by mail, a custom practiced for other types of needlework.[18]

The quilting bee was an integral part of the quilt's place in the social structure. The "bee," as its name implies, is a communal work project. Americans had many bees: harvesting, corn-husking, house- and barn-raising, and, of course, quilting. Large-scale work projects such as harvesting and erecting structures could go on for several days, with food contributed by participants or those benefiting from the pooled labor. In the days when distances between neighbors was greater, and transportation slow and difficult, workers and their families stayed overnight, often sleeping in their wagons or in tents. Alice Earle in *Home Life in Colonial Days* mentions a Narragansett quilting bee in 1752 which went on for ten days, most likely one to which local women returned each day.[19] Usually, however, they lasted a day, and were as much communal festivity as shared labor, a characteristic of most bees. After the work of the day, typically, there was celebration, common food preparation and feasting, dancing, courting, games, much consumption of hard beverages, all of those festivities which characterized rural American social life. In 1895 Alice Earle talked to a New England farmer's wife who admitted that she didn't get too lonely as long as there were enough quiltings during the year. The previous winter there had been twenty-eight "regular" bees, and besides those she had done her own piecing and helped neighbors informally with quilting projects.[20]

The indefatigable Ruth Henshaw Bascomb, whose primitive portraits are well known, recounted in her journal, now in the possession of the American Antiquarian Society, her life from the age of seventeen until her death in 1847. Catherine Fennelly comments on the journal:

Often there were quiltings, either at the homes of neighbors or in their own kitchen and sitting room. "This afternoon 21 young ladies paid us a visit and assisted us in quilting"—on this occasion on Mrs. Henshaw's petticoat. It took four days, with some assistance, to prepare and quilt a coat for Mrs. Scott. A printed India cotton coverlet had to have a backing made for it, then must be quilted. A patchwork coverlet was quilted in three days; "evening a large number of gentlemen." Another, made shortly before Ruth's marriage, was striped in plaid and plain "tea color" calico (dyed by Ruth herself), then quilted in two days; two piecework bed quilts took six days to complete with outside help. One quilt was completed in two days, Ruth and a friend sewing during the day, six neighbors helping in the evening. At the same time one of these quiltings was taking place, the men of the family held a husking bee.[21]

This gives some indication of the time it would take to make and complete quilts; other estimates of the time it took to make the quilt top and do the final quilting are difficult to find.[22] In Pennsylvania, according to Frances Lichten:

Quilts intended for everyday use were made in simple designs of squares, diamonds, or narrow strips, for these practical women wasted no unnecessary stitchery on objects destined to be impermanent. If, however, they were meant for keepsakes or were planned as an outlet for love of color and a release for nervous energy, then the work expended on them became a pure labor of love. Sometimes all the spare time of several years was occupied in piecing or in appliquéing one set of quilt blocks. . . . Quilting was an occupation usually saved for the winter months, when the daily farm work made fewer demands on the housewife. . . . Out came the quilting frames to be set up in a warm corner of the house. If it was an everyday quilt, there were no needlework flourishes to eat up extra hours. In the spare time of one or two days, a woman finished a simple quilt and got the bulky frames out of the way, for they took up considerable space when in use.[23]

Since a quilting bee was an important social as well as work event, great care was taken by the woman whose house was to be the site of activity. "For it, the floors were scoured and sanded, and things in general brought into perfect order. Pies, cakes, preserves, and Hyson tea, with large lumps of loaf sugar, were provided liberally for the occasion."[24] Recalling a quilting party in a New England town of 1815, Elias Nason wrote that the women "arrange their dresses at the . . . looking-glass, and then seat themselves in the flag-bottomed chairs, prepared with scissors, thimbles, thread and needles for the work before them."[25]

Four or more women, seated around the intimate space of the frame, their hands busy, had what must have been delightful hours to discuss the affairs of the region.

The conversation, as well might be supposed—for the public library, lyceum, railroad, telegraph and telephone had not then appeared—was not very aesthetical, literary, scientific, or instructive. The women of that period, in the rural village I am thinking of, had but little time to read, or to think of much, except domestic and church affairs, together with the faults and foibles of their friends and neighbors. . . . So, as the busy needles pierce the quilt, the busy tongues, sharp as the needles, pierce the characters of the absent.[26]

Women who feared for their reputation never failed to answer invitations to a quilting.[27] So the traditional lore says, the juiciest gossip was saved for the time when the quilt, rolled up as it was worked, was reduced to a small rectangle, and the women's heads closest together. A story, "The Quilting at Miss Jones's," in *Godey's,* January 1868, describes a quilting party—in country dialect:

Our minister was married a year ago, and we have been piecing him a bed quilt; and last week we quilted it. I always make a pint of going to quiltings, for you can't be backbited to your face, that's a moral sertenty . . . quiltin' just set wim-

men to slanderin' as easy and beautiful as everything you ever see'. So I went. There wasn't anybody there when I got there. For reason, I always go early. . . . The quilt was made of different kinds of calico; all the wimmen round had pieced a block or two, and we took up a collection to get the batten and linin', and the cloth to set it together with, which was turkey red, and come to quilt it it looked well; we quilted it herrin'-bone, and a runnin' vine 'round the border. After [,] the path-master was demorelized, the school-mistress tore to pieces, the party to Ripleys scandelized, Miss Brown's baby voted a unquestionable idiot, and the rest of the unrepresented neighborhood dealt with. . . .[28]

Most likely the frame would have been set up beforehand, and the quilt put in. There were many methods of drawing quilting patterns. Long straight lines were ruled with a straight edge, or could be made with a carpenter's line, a chalked string, stretched tight across, then snapped to leave its mark. Templates of cardboard or tin were made, and traced around. In Pennsylvania, patterns of tin, looking like cookie cutters, were dipped in starch and pressed on the quilt, the dried starch leaving a line which could be followed but would wash out. Designs were drawn on free-hand, or common objects, such as plates and cups were used to trace out circles and other shapes. Katheryne Travis mentions a lady in the Ozarks who said: ". . . now this here quiltin', well I jes' went out in the yard and got some leaves off the rosebush and laid 'em down and drawed around them, and made my own quiltin' pattern."[29] Really expert quilters disdained leaving any such marks of their patterns, and pricked out their designs with a needle.

Quilting patterns are of particular interest to us as they may relate to the overall design. They are a separate study in themselves, but I will briefly sketch a few general trends. Quilting patterns are of course either in straight or curved lines and the geometric and representational figures they can form; among the latter are flowers, hearts, feathers, and birds. While there are many quilts with straightlined forms only, those with exclusively curved-line forms are quite rare; they are harder to do. Generally, both will be combined in a single quilt. The most flamboyant quilting generally is seen on plain quilts, which are really a canvas for quilting patterns. There was highly elaborate curvilinear quilting used on English and American clothes and coverlets of the seventeenth and eighteenth centuries, some of it "corded" quilting, in which a cord is inserted between top and bottom layers of cloth in a channel prepared for it by sewing parallel lines, giving a raised, edged effect. Such elaborate work was applicable to plain covers, on which it was employed, but obviously not to pieced or appliqué quilts, where it would have obscured the designs formed by the patchwork.

For pieced quilts there evolved a grid pattern, simply parallel lines running diagonally each way across the quilt. This style can be seen on early American pieced quilts; the majority we have examined of the eighteenth and early nineteenth centuries have similar straight-lined quilting patterns. Here, as in England, the elaborate quilting was more regularly employed on plain quilts, such as the linsey-woolsey, and the plain all-white linen and cotton quilts. More elaborate quilting on patchwork quilts was introduced on the borders of the central-medallion-style covers; then, especially in America, as designs opened up and the block-style emerged, intricate quilting was used in areas of the quilt not taken up with pieced or appliqué patterns. The use of open squares interspersed with pieced blocks left perfect areas for fine quilting, and into these would go wreaths, flowers, hearts. Borders and separating strips between blocks also offered areas for elaborate quilting. Appliqué patterns tend to leave more open space than pieced, and, because of their curvilinear forms and status as "best" quilts, often have a higher percentage of lavish quilting in baroque forms. Such quilting designs were independent of the patchwork patterns; quilting was also done which emphasized the pieced and appliqué designs. Where pieced quilts were composed of linked blocks, quilting patterns often followed the inside edges of the pieces which formed the patterns; for example, in a Log Cabin quilt the quilting will often follow the lines of the "logs," and any curved or more elaborate quilting would be on the open border areas. This was largely a matter of convenience; the lines of the pieces could be followed without the necessity of drawing quilting lines and it avoided the difficult task of sewing over seams. More intentional effects were produced by following the lines of patchwork pieces out into the neutral areas which might have surrounded them; an example of this is shown in figure 31, and an example of quilting which is done within the block to emphasize form is shown in plate 31, a quilt from Colorado, in which circular quilting follows the lines of the block pattern. In general, it is the rarer pieced quilt in which the quilting is used to emphasize design, but where this is done it is generally quite effective, giving an extra-dimensional effect to the patterns.

In "The Quilting at Miss Jones's," quoted earlier, page 87, the speaker referred to "batten"—batting—the filler of the quilt. By the time the story was written, in 1868, cotton was the common filling for quilts, though wool would be used where extra warmth was needed, or if for some reason there was no access to cotton. If wool was used to make a thick quilt or comforter, it would often be tufted (tied through) in spots rather than quilted because of the difficulty of forcing a needle through such thick padding. Cotton was used for filling quilts as early as the mid-sixteenth century in England. But it was a rare commodity in the early days of settlement in the United States. Though cotton had been planted in America in the seventeenth century, it was evidently more an ornamental plant than a serious crop until well into the eighteenth. Up until the Revolution, wadding for quilts was imported from England. Cotton was difficult to use because

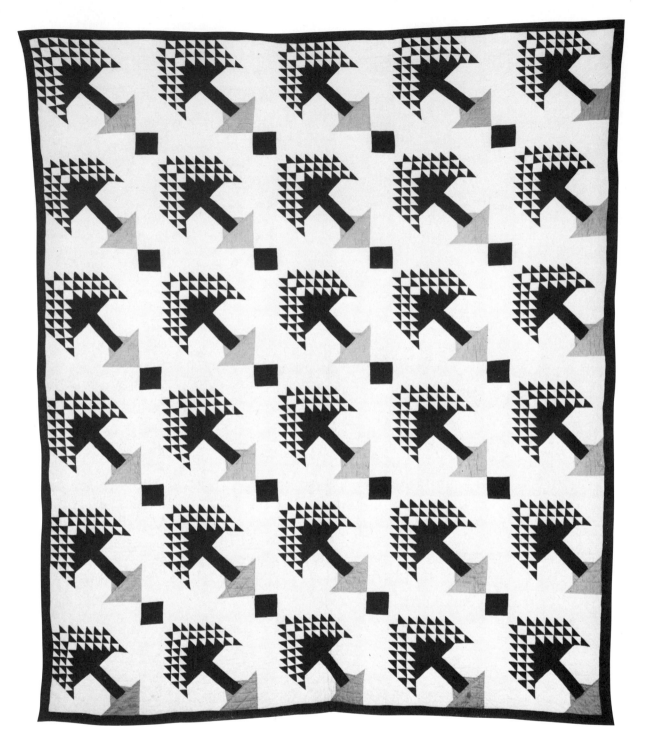

of its seeds and inevitable foreign matter, and required laborious hand-cleaning; some early Southern quilts used it, the cotton picked clean by slave labor. A little native raw cotton was evidently also used in the North, but was not favored until the invention of the cotton gin eliminated the hand-cleaning process. The surmise is, therefore, that most early American quilts used wool which would have been more readily available and cheaper than cotton. This may also be true for

Figure 31. Pine Tree. New York, c. 1910. 70″ x 64″. The symbol of the pine was a favorite one in colonial New England, used on its coinage, standards—and quilts. This old pattern has been used for several centuries without change. (Rhea Goodman, Quilt Gallery, Inc.)

Figure 32. Lady of the Lake. New England, c. 1890. 73½″ x 73″. Although regularly organized, the pattern breaks up visually, kept in motion by the directional impact of the dark triangles. There is a large eight-pointed star formed in the design.

England; the broadside, "The Case of the Quilt-Makers" (see Appendix), mentions the use of short strands of wool for stuffing. Mavis FitzRandolph, speaking of English quilting, says: "Any quilt or quilted garment made before 1800 which I have been able to examine is padded with sheep's wool."[30] Wool was more readily available and cheaper until the advent of the cotton gin and the great industry it sparked made cotton an inexpensive and common commodity.

Dimensions of quilts vary widely, often a clue to their age, since particular sizes of beds were popular in different periods. The earliest quilts which have survived are usually of large size, as big as ten feet square, to cover the high, wide beds of the time. The three-quarter-size bed which became popular in the first quarter of the nineteenth century accounts for the oddly sized quilts of that period. The small Victorian silk crazy quilts were usually meant only for ornament or throws, so were not big enough to give any effective coverage.

I have set aside Pennsylvania for some particular comments because of its unique place in American quilt history. From the German settlers in Pennsylvania sprang some of the most interesting and visually moving of America's eighteenth-, nineteenth-, and twentieth-century pieced quilts.

Pennsylvania had in its fertile middle land a large population of closely knit settlers, of similar backgrounds and predilections, who maintained—and maintain to this day—a distinctive life style. Of a number of Protestant sects (Mennonites and their Amish offshoot, Moravians, Lutherans), they had in common their deep commitment to Christian living and practice as against theoretical and intellectualized religion. Some loved fancy folk decoration, others were "plain," avoiding decoration in their clothing and surroundings. All loved color. They were craftsmen as well as farmers, and maintained self-sufficient farms and communities through which they could satisfy most of their material, and spiritual, needs. Their craft and art, although owing much to European models, changed in response to the new environment just as did the art of other transplanted groups. But it remained unmistakably and quintessentially Pennsylvania German. They were, and are, pious, hard-working, frugal, fundamentalist in religion, and maintain a body of folk images and artistic ideas, perhaps less changed in their sojourn in the New World than those of any other group. Their skillful farming, continual labor, and thriftiness have made them relatively prosperous and enabled them to maintain their way of life to a rather remarkable degree; they accommodate the changing world as little as possible.

To this day tourists delight in the Amish and the Reformed Mennonites, appearing in their buggies on county roads, clothed in somber colors, the Amish men in their prescribed wide-brimmed hats, their eschewal of buttons on their outer clothing a symbol of their rejection of the military. They use no electricity, thus have no radios or television, allow nothing solely for decoration in their homes, and work their farms by horse and hand. They carry no insurance, and use no lightning rods on their buildings. If a barn burns, the entire community gives aid both manual and financial, if necessary, to replace it. Others, less strict, drive cars with the chrome carefully painted out, dress in conservative fashion, women often wearing caps in the same style as those worn by their ancestors in northern Europe. Members of the other Protestant groups, whose lives are not circumscribed by such restrictions as the Amish employ, have contributed many of the colorful folk arts of Pennsylvania.

Quilts always have been an important part of all Pennsylvania German households, and their women's work. "Never content with her stock, she was continually preoccupied with the planning of new and better quilts. The need to provide a dowry of such stuffs for each marriageable daughter and son and to pile up a

Figure 33. Basket of Scraps. Pennsylvania, c. 1860. Cotton. 91" x 75". A variation of the Basket pattern—the block pieced of thirteen parts: six triangles, two rectangles, one square, and four diamonds.

Figure 34 (far left). Centered square. Amish. Pennsylvania, c. 1870. Wool. 80" x 73". Pieced quilts do not come much simpler than this. The colors are gray and brown, a plain quilt done by plain people, but a very powerful image.

Figure 35 (left). Single inside border. Amish. Ohio, c. 1940. Cotton. 83" x 59". An inside rectangle formed by strips of a contrasting color. The Amish excelled at working such simplified formats in conjunction with rich colors.

store of quilts for the future use of the family remaining under the home roof-tree kept her fingers perennially busy. . . ."[31]

Early Pennsylvania German settlers used featherbeds, the custom obviously brought with them from northern Europe; ". . . quilts were thrown over the great tickings filled with goose feathers, which kept all the German settlers warm in the winter time."[32] They were used in their inns; this from the New Englander Elkanah Watson, on his stay in a Reamstown Inn in 1777: "I was placed between two beds, without sheets or pillows. This, I was told, was the prevailing custom, but which, as far as my experience goes, tends little to promote sleep or comfort of a stranger."[33] And this from another New England traveler, this time a girl, who commented on her stay in an inn in Berks County in 1810: "Our bed to sleep on was straw & then a feather bed for covering—The pillows contain'd nearly a single handful of feathers, & were cover'd with the most curious & dirty patchwork, I ever saw—We had one bed quilt & one sheet."[34]

Some thirty-five years later, Phebe Gibbons, the daughter of a prominent Philadelphia Quaker, who had married Dr. Joseph Gibbons, moved to Bird-in-Hand in Lancaster County, in the heart of Pennsylvania German country. Her essays on the rural life around her were keenly observed and retain their freshness; this is her section on "Quiltings" in an essay on the Pennsylvania Germans:

Some ten years ago there came to our neighborhood a pleasant, industrious "Aunt Sally" . . . and the other day she had a quilting for she had long wished to

Figure 36 (above, left). Single inside border with corners. Amish. Pennsylvania, c. 1920. Wool. 74″ x 74″. Another variation of the inside border idea—this one with the block corners seen on many Amish quilts.

Figure 37 (above, right). Double inside border. Amish. Ohio, c. 1940. Cotton. 79″ x 69″. The colors are navy blue and russet; the superb quilting is typical of Amish quilts.

recover two quilts. The first neighbor who arrived at Aunt Sally's was our neighbor from over the "creek" or mill-stream, Polly M., in her black silk Mennist bonnet, formed like a sun-bonnet; and at ten came my dear friend Susanna E., who is tall and fat, and very pleasant; . . . Aunt Sally had her quilt up in her landlord's east room, for her own house was too small. However, at about eleven she called us over to dinner; for people who have breakfasted at five or six have an appetite at eleven. . . .

After dinner came our next neighbors, "the maids," Sally and Katy Groff, who live in single blessedness and great neatness. [The Pennsylvania quilt in plate 65 is signed "Mary Groff 1873."] They wore pretty, clear-starched Mennist caps, very plain. Katy is a sweet-looking woman, and although she is more than sixty years old, her forehead is almost unwrinkled, and her fine hair is still brown. It was late when the farmer's wife came—three o'clock, for she had been to Lancaster. She wore hoops, and was of the "world's people." These women all spoke "Dutch" [sic], for "the maids," whose ancestors came here probably one hundred and fifty years ago, do not speak English with fluency yet.

The first subject of conversation was the fall house-cleaning; and I heard mention of "die carpett hinans an der fence," and "die fenshter und die porch," and the exclamation, "My goodness, es war schlimm." I quilted faster than Katy Groff, who showed me her hands, and said, "You have not been corn-husking, as I have."

So we quilted and rolled, talked and laughed, got one quilt done, and put in *another. The work was not fine; we laid it out by chalking around a small plate. Aunt Sally's desire was rather to get her quilting finished upon this occasion, than for us to put in a quantity of needlework.*

About five o'clock we were called to supper. I will not tell you all the particulars of this plentiful meal. But the stewed chicken was tender, and we had coffee again.

Polly M.'s husband now came over the creek in the boat, to take her home, and he warned her against the evening dampness. The rest of us quilted awhile by candle and lamp, and got the second quilt done at about seven.

At this quilting there was little gossip, and less scandal. I displayed my new alpaca, and my dyed merino, and the Philadelphia bonnet which exposes the back of my head to the wintry blast. Polly, for her part, preferred a black silk sun-bonnet; and so we parted, with mutual invitations to visit.[35]

Pennsylvania quilts are distinctive. Their appliqué designs use many motifs derived from their German background—hearts, peacocks, tulips—found on furniture and other household furnishings. While they shared many block designs with other areas of the country, they had some unique variations on the well-known designs, and some designs distinctly their own. But it is in the area of color invention that they excelled, and in which their pieced quilts are most distinctive.

The Pennsylvania Germans love color. They lavish it on their houses and possessions, plant it in their gardens.

In addition to being beautifully tidy, a property will be made as colorful as its owner's ingenuity can devise, for the love of strong color is still a dominant passion in the Pennsylvania Germans. . . . In their use of color there is no restraint or repression. The eye of the Pennsylvania German would be starved by the white, black and green of New England, and the grey and white of the lovely stone houses of the English settlers in the State were as little to his taste. When a farmhouse of this type came into his possession, he enlivened its Quaker coloring by any means at hand, for in its original state he thought it cold and repellent. . . . Not for these rural folk are the subtle shades, those to be found in floral hybrids—the delicate mauves, off-yellows, faint pinks and lilacs, for they consider them "washed out," a term they would apply to fabrics of the same hues.[36]

No New Englander or Southerner would juxtapose the intense pink with the deep red and pastel blues and greens of the Amish Central Diamond quilt of

Plate 32. Bars. Amish. Pennsylvania, c. 1925. Wool. 84" x 76". One of the several formats unique to the Amish, a bordered central panel of bars. This design is similar in impact to the central-diamond style. (Rhea Goodman, Quilt Gallery, Inc.)

plate 35. The Pennsylvania Germans managed a playful manipulation of form and color in their quilts which to earlier writers seemed discordant:

Only a soul in desperate need of nervous outlet could have conceived and executed . . . the "Full Blown Tulip" [which she illustrates], a quilt of Pennsylvania Dutch origin. It is a perfect accomplishment from a needlework standpoint yet hideous. The "tulip" block is composed of eight arrow-shaped patches of· brilliant purplish red; the eight petal-shaped patches inserted between the red arrows are a sickly lemon yellow. The center of each tulip is made of the material used for setting the blocks together—homespun of the most terrifying shade of brownish green, beyond question the accident of a private dyepot. . . . The whole is surrounded by a second border . . . of dazzlingly bright orange. The green-red-lemon-orange combination is enough to set a blind man's teeth on edge. . . . And yet as an example of needlework it is a triumph.[37]

She describes a not atypical Pennsylvania quilt, the color combination perhaps more agreeable to contemporary eyes. Pennsylvania women used colors, of maximum intensity in their quilts, often combining them in a way which sounds impossible in verbal description, but, simply, "works" in actuality.

It must be said that our acceptance of these combinations is perhaps conditioned by the color usages of contemporary art and design; but it is my feeling that they represent a sure grasp of the possibilities of strong contrast worked out in the absence of any adherence to established outer "taste." While these quilts lack the serenity of a dignified New England or New York quilt of subdued and carefully modulated hues, they have a unique and gay aggressiveness in color that reflects the Pennsylvania German zest for strong and fundamental living. Food is simple and served in abundance; jokes are broad; their relationship to God and His Word direct. There is a rich, shared, and satisfying spiritual and physical life which is true still to their foundings in elemental Christian beliefs; their quilts reflect their gaiety of spirit.

I have put together in the plates a number of Amish quilts which illustrate their manipulation of color and form within the limits of a simple pattern. The Amish now make quilts which are indistinguishable from those of their non-Amish neighbors; but there is a large, distinct body of quilts similar in design to those I have illustrated which are in their traditional styles. They are made in a limited range of designs, usually of wool; some of the designs are of ancient and common use, others are unique to the Amish. I point out, in the latter case, the straight barred quilts of plates 32 and 33, and the central diamond quilts of plates 34 and 35. These Amish diamond quilts should be compared to the linsey-woolsey quilt

Plate 33. Bars. Amish. Pennsylvania, c. 1930. Wool. 79″ x 74″. A typical variation of a common theme, such Amish quilts depend on color manipulation and proportional changes of the elements in a given format. (Collection of Sarah Melvin)

Plate 34. Diamond. Amish. Pennsylvania, c. 1920. Wool. 78" x 76". A favorite Amish format, the central diamond, most likely a remnant of the central-medallion-style quilt. There is often little variance between one maker's work and the next, except in color. (Collection of Bill Gallick and Tony Ellis)

Plate 35. Diamond. Amish. Pennsylvania, c. 1930. Wool. 87" x 83". This quilt and that in plate 34 demonstrate the grounding of Amish quilts in color rather than form invention. Typically, there is a thin outer border in a contrasting color. (Collection of Bill Gallick and Tony Ellis)

from the same state, figure 18, discussed earlier; it is possible that they are a late-surviving example of that simplified rendition of the central-medallion style; the conservatism of the Amish would account for this retention of an earlier format. Other favored patterns are the checkerboard grid of Around the World, called by them Sunshine and Shadow, and borders enclosing just a large field of color (also unique to them). While piecing is almost invariably by machine, the quilting is by hand and usually superb. What is most interesting is their use of color variations on these repeated themes. They are startling, the hot magentas, blues, greens, reds—an erotic spectrum—especially when we compare them to the subdued life style of the Amish. The answer to this seeming dilemma is that these colors are used under their cloaks and in their homes, in their skirts, blouses, shirts, once of fine wools, and now of wools, cottons, synthetics, but still in the same vibrant colors. Phebe Gibbons spoke in 1872 of seeing some Amish women at a railroad station; one had a "gray shawl . . . brown stuff dress, purple apron. One young girl wore a bright-brown sun-bonnet, a green dress, and a light blue apron." In her essay, "An Amish Meeting," she said: "The women, whom I have sometimes seen with a bright-purple apron, an orange neckerchief, or some other striking bit of color, were now more soberly arrayed in plain white caps without ruffle or border, and white neckerchiefs, though occasionally a cap or kerchief was black."[38]

Naturally enough, the scraps from clothesmaking and good parts of used clothing would end up as quilt parts, and if they wished to use whole cloth for a quilt, they often picked these colors. While the colors and their combinations are startling, they are not bright in the manner of the brilliantly colored Pennsylvania cotton quilts; rather, they are deep and saturated colors, even somber, which in combination, especially in the wools, glow with what often seems like an inner fire; they are often reminiscent of the Delaunays' palettes. The lack of patterned materials in most of these quilts reflects the Amish rejection of such patterned fabrics in their clothes, though some simply patterned textiles can be used in household furnishings. The Amish dress in a limited, but intense range of colors, and these quilts reflect that; almost any combination works, but, of course, some work better than others. The sometimes neon-like effects are usually those of later quilts, made of wool combinations or synthetics which are now used probably because they are closest in feel to the older fine wools.

The number of plates in this book devoted to Pennsylvania quilts reflects my obvious interest in the sorts of color and form manipulations the Pennsylvania Germans practiced so well.

Plate 36. Diamond. Amish. Pennsylvania, c. 1915. Wool. 84″ x 84″. The Amish diamond
format, without block corners—just the calm geometry of large diamonds and squares,
in deep wool colors, the essence of Amish sensibilities. (America Hurrah Antiques. N.Y.C.)

Plate 37. Nine-Patch Block. Amish. Pennsylvania, c. 1900. Wool. 83″ x 72″. An elegant Nine-Patch showing typical Amish restraint; the large corners are a feature of a majority of their quilts.

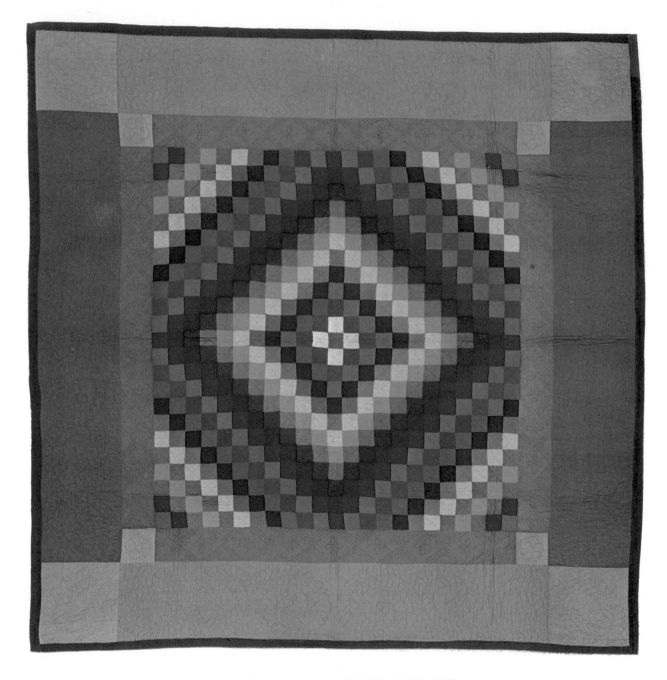

Plate 38. Sunshine and Shadow. Amish. Pennsylvania, c. 1930. Wool. 76″ x 74″.
Others call this Trip Around the World, but to the Amish it is always Sunshine and
Shadow. It has been a popular pattern since the turn of the century.
(Collection of Sarah Melvin)

Plate 39. Sunshine and Shadow. Amish. Pennsylvania, c. 1930. Wool. 80″ x 80″.
The border here is of the deep red wool that the Amish have used for a century or
more. (America Hurrah Antiques, N.Y.C.)

Plate 40. Sawtooth. Amish. Pennsylvania, c. 1930. Cotton. 87½" x 87½". The Amish use cottons and, more recently, synthetics in the same color ranges as their wools. Sawtooth-edged patterns are quite uncommon. (Collection of Sarah Melvin)

Plate 41. Baskets or Cake Stand. Amish. Pennsylvania, c. 1940. Wool. 80" x 80". A popular Amish pattern, here with the baskets in a glowing pink. (Collection of Sarah Melvin)

Plate 42. Log Cabin—Barn Raising. Amish. Pennsylvania, c. 1900. Wool. 78″ x 77″.
Although the colors are basically Amish, the use of patterned material is not. The
blocks have been carefully planned to produce the overall effect.

Plate 43. Streak of Lightning. Amish. Pennsylvania, c. 1910. Wool. 73″ x 71″. As in
most Amish quilts, the simplest means are used for maximum effect; here, bold steps
of black and red contained in a wide green border of just the right shade.

Plate 44. Log Cabin—Straight Furrow. Amish. Pennsylvania, c. 1925. Wool and
worsted. 75″ x 72″. Showing the usual Amish color sense, the blocks were
assembled from a number of different materials, but all in the same tonalities. Log
Cabin quilts, while common in Pennsylvania, are rarely made by the Amish.

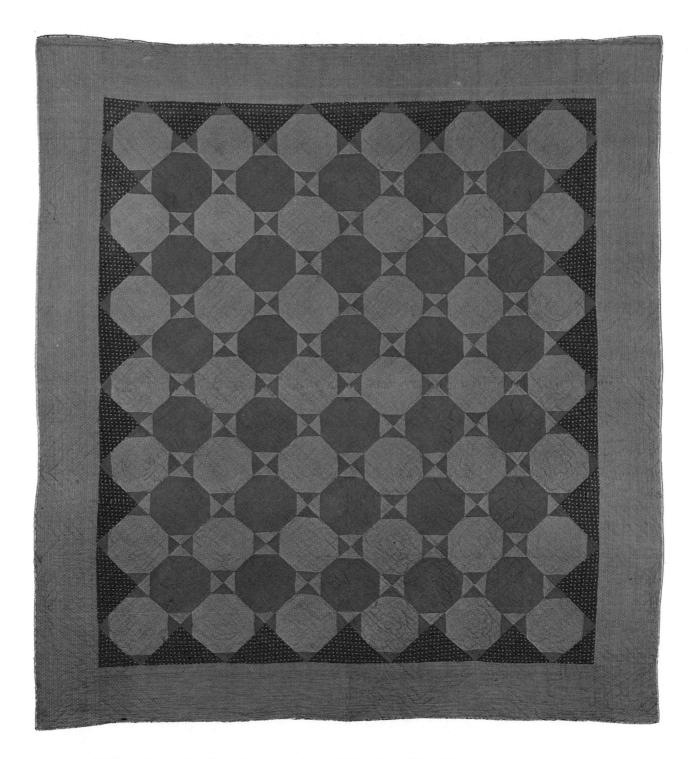

Plate 45. Robbing Peter to Pay Paul. Pennsylvania, c. 1870. Cotton. 85″ x 81″.
Also called Lend and Borrow, and always in two colors, both pattern names come
from the mechanics of making the pattern—scraps from cutting the color for
one block become part of the design elements of the other.

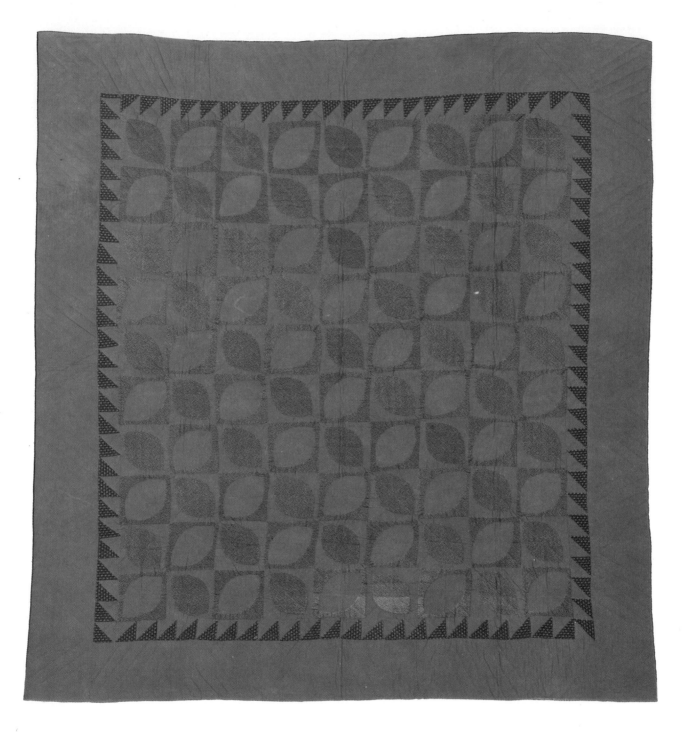

6 The Skilled Hand, The Practiced Eye

The often startling resemblances between the total visual effects of some pieced quilts and certain examples of modern painting are intriguing. Some of the more obvious areas of comparison would include:

—That manipulation of geometric form which has characterized the work of many painters since the advent of Abstractionism.

—The optical effects of such quilts as Baby Blocks, plate 50, and the work of Vasarely and others who have explored the possibilities of various modes of retinal stimulation through color and form relationships, optical illusion, manipulations of linear effects.

—The use of repeated images drawn from the environment, as in the Coffee Cups quilt, plate 51, and the sequential use of images in the work of such artists as Andy Warhol.

—The repetitive use of highly reduced geometric forms, as in figure 34, and the work of the systemic painters.

—The color variations on a single format, as in the Amish quilts, and such paintings as Albers' *Homage to the Square* series.

—The manipulation for visual effect of chromatic possibilities in a geometric framework as in such quilts as Rainbow quilts, and the work of such painters as Kenneth Noland.

   No matter how striking the similarities, however, it is obvious that the quilts did not look like paintings when they were made. If, indeed, such designs had been transferred to canvas and presented as paintings (such, of course, was not possible, for there was no established aesthetic, or groundwork, for "high" art objects of such an appearance), they would have been, at the least, reviled. Yet such designs commonly appeared amid the Victorian clutter, as illustrated in the stereoscope card discussed previously. It is obvious that quilts, and other objects which now seem to us "modern" in appearance, were accepted in their times as common, utilitarian objects which did not carry the implications of "art." It was not until certain developments had taken place in cultural history though, that these objects would be called back from the kitchen, workshop, and rural home for general reconsideration. What had occurred between the time many

Plate 46. Melon Patch. Pennsylvania, c. 1885. Cotton 80″ x 76″. A fantastic color combination which, as with so many unusually hued Pennsylvania quilts, manages to work in a cohesive manner.

of these quilts were made and mid-twentieth century was the emergence of geometric form as a consciously employed primary source in design, painting, and sculpture. Geometry, as we have seen, was implicit in the ageless tradition of functional design in household objects, in tools, and in machines. Plato said in *Philebus:* "By beauty of shapes I do not mean, as most people would suppose, the beauty of living figures or of pictures, but, to make my point clear, I mean straight lines and circles, and shapes, plane or solid, made from them by lathe, ruler and square. These are not, like other things, beautiful relatively, but always and absolutely." Plato's theory was echoed in Cézanne's famous statement: "You must see in nature the cylinder, the sphere and the cone," and his work was to influence deeply the development of Cubism, in which the nature of objects in terms of their geometry, planes, lines, and basic forms, was investigated. The Cubists' formulations in turn had a profound effect on the art of the later twentieth century.

The Bauhaus, instrumental in the formation of the "modern" style, established the rule of geometry in design as a theoretical necessity. Such painters associated with the Bauhaus as Josef Albers carried the implications of geometry as an abstract style in painting to logical ends; his geometric abstractions, particularly the *Homage to the Square* series, chromatic variations on squares-within-squares, the painting varying in size but identical in format, have had an important effect on American art of the past several decades, ranging from "op art," which depends on optical effects produced through the manipulation of line, color, and form in geometric formats, to systemic painting, characterized by "extremely simplified forms, usually of a geometric character, either in a single concentrated image configuration or in serial runs or sets."[1]

It is obviously well beyond the scope of this discussion to trace cohesively or fully the influence of geometry on twentieth-century painting and design. Nor have I illustrated examples of those modern paintings which are strikingly similar to some quilts. I wish merely to indicate the pervasiveness of its influence. "The non-objective artist eagerly invaded every aspect of life and . . . succeeded in revolutionizing our environment in an amazingly short time. Skyscrapers, linoleum, magazine layouts, lamps, even the mirrors in restaurant rest-rooms . . . all take their streamlined angles because such men as Van Doesburg insisted that art must act on everything."[2] "One of the ironies of modern art will be the refusal of a child in 1982 to see anything in a Mondrian but the façade of a famous building."[3]

Thus we have become attuned to accepting the design of these as "modern"; and those objects made in the past whose design is similarly based on primary forms also appear "contemporary" to us. In the case particularly of pieced quilts, the quiltmaking technique predicated the use of geometry in their design, and long experimentation produced a great variety of both complex and simple forms. Their colors, from dyed materials, ranged equally from the primary spectrum of such painters as Mondrian to the subtle modulation which can be seen in the work of such painters as Albers and Noland, and it would appear that quiltmakers arrived at many visual results similar to those obtained by artists painting as much as a century later.

Other factors increase the resemblance between quilts and paintings. First, quilts have the same format as most paintings; that is, they are rectangular or square. Obviously, this is because the beds they were made for were rectangular. The rectangle for reasons of structural efficiency is perhaps the most pervasive man-made form in our culture. Painters fitted their frescoes to largely squared interiors and exteriors, worked on squared panels, affixed their canvases to rectangular stretchers. And quiltmakers shaped their products to the forms of their beds. The second coincidence is size; the move to the large canvas in contemporary painting produced works which by chance coincided in general dimensions with surviving quilts. Quilt size was, of course, determined by bed size; the movement there was from larger to smaller—the modern "king-size" bed approaching again the dimensions of the "great" beds of the past. One other similarity to be noted is that most objects we find in the tradition of vernacular, functional design are three-dimensional, sculptural in appearance. Quilts are flat or two-dimensional, as are paintings.

Intriguing and startling as these resemblances may be, however, any direct linking of the two mediums would be demeaning to the history and presence of both quilts and paintings. Implicit in the act of creating a painting is the intellectual process which ties the work of an artist to his aesthetic ancestors and his peers, and places it in the history of objects specifically made to be art. This is precisely the quality which was absent in the making of pieced quilts.[4] The women who made pieced quilts were not "artists," that is, they did not intend to make art, had no sense of the place of their work in a continuous stream of art history, did not, in short, intellectualize the production of handcraft any more than did the makers of objects in the vernacular tradition the world over. Usually quilts are classed with American "folk" or "primitive" art. They do, of course, spring from the same milieu and sensibilities which produced such work; but the classification is very imprecise as it includes functional objects ranging from painted tinware to decoys, and earthenware jugs to door hinges; objects whose formal basis is painting or sculpture but whose intent is functional (tavern signs and weathervanes); and "naive" painting, drawing, and sculpture. "Naive" implies the maker's unawareness of formal principles of composition, rendering, and the like. Aesthetic problems are handled directly and intuitively rather than academically, and the best folk art of all kinds shows an innate awareness of the force and value of basic forms; in folk painting and sculpture form is emphasized beyond the niceties of perspective, accurate detail, and so on. Strictly speaking, some decorative content is implied in the term "folk art"; utilitarian articles of simple beauty, without embellishment, would more correctly be placed in the category of the vernacular tradition of functional design. Pieced quilts occupy an unusual position: they are decorative products of the folk milieu, the basis of whose decoration was a functional technique, and thus they fall also into the vernacular design tradition. In other words, the design or embellishment of a pieced quilt is its top, but the top itself is a functional solution to the problem of making inexpensive bedding from available materials. Quiltmakers consciously manipulated the technique to make visually meaningful and moving surfaces.

Many functional objects which appear to us abstractly "beautiful" may be so without intent; made to answer need and function rather than taste, their volumes, forms, and lines appear without embellishment in the beauty of the geometry enunciated by Plato. Pieced quilts were meant to be beautiful. In addition to making the most functional bedcover possible in her home, the craftsman wrought her tops consciously, thoughtfully, and with great skill and invention, to appeal to the eye. This itself was done in a functional manner; that is, the block-style pieced top was the most efficient combination of available materials and time to produce a needed object. Their geometric style is the natural outcome of the most rational construction-modular possible for their purposes—the square and its divisions—which could be crafted without elaborate tools or technical knowledge.

Thus, while they did not consciously exploit geometry as idealized form, quiltmakers used the format which experimentation had shown to be the most felicitous to their aims. Pieced quilts are the most "painterly" products of the vernacular tradition, both in appearance because of the use of geometric elements and abstract images, rectangular format, size, and flatness, and in decorative technique: quiltmakers, in effect, "paint" with fabrics, choosing first a format and ultimate look they want, then selecting colors, patterns, and textures among their available materials, their "palette," and manipulating these elements in conjunction with form to achieve the effect they wish. While they decidedly are not paintings in the formal sense, their method and design can best be described through comparisons to that medium.

Like paintings, pieced quilts have marked stylistic periods, a history of aesthetic development, which can be traced and described. The majority of objects made in the vernacular traditions are extremely slow to change in style, often looking the same century after century. However, that vernacular tradition of quiltmaking early colonists brought to this country was greatly accelerated by the conditions of American life; a new environment with new demands, and the self-confidence and openness with which Americans approached their environment and national destiny, created a milieu in which inventiveness and new solutions were searched for and prized. This situation is paralleled by the development within the American milieu, after long subservience to European modes, of a distinctly American painting style; here, too, an increase in self-confidence and a slower but equally significant break with the past engendered new aesthetic models. Pieced quilts progress from an Old World to a New World style, from the central-medallion quilt to the block-style; aesthetic development followed the new style, from the first production of block-style pieced quilts which borrowed elements from "high style" quilts to the celebration and elaboration of those elements as an end and a new model. There were sharp regional differences: color ranged from the vividness of Pennsylvania German quilts to the often more sombre hues of those of New England; form ranged from the elegant and simplified formats of the Amish to the intricate, sharp-edged designs of Long Island and Maine to the open, naturalistic abstractions of the Ohio Valley. The appearance of quilts was deeply affected by the feeling and fashion of the era in which they were made. In a gay and expansive era, citizens dressed themselves and their homes in rich, bold colors and patterns, and quilts, made from fashion's scraps, shared the feeling; in periods of doubt and distress, or financial disaster, fashion retreated and so did quilts. (As an example of the latter, quilts made during the Depression, even though they are based on the same patterns as those made before and after that frightening period, and are equally well stitched, are recessive, the colors rarely assertive or gay. The Around the World quilt, plate 55, is an example of this.)

Different textures, dyes, and types of materials handle light differently, affecting the look of the quilt. Finely woven cottons and silks are in general more reflective than wool, velvet, corduroy, coarsely woven cotton. The Irish Chain quilt (plate 57) used solid wool centers bounded by the lines of cotton squares; the different ways the two materials reflect light gives the quilt added dimensionality, the solid reds appearing to recede. The chevron-patterned quilt with a crazy center (plate 58) exploits the reflective contrasts between silks and velvets, and illustrates the Victorian fondness for gorgeous effects. The Ocean Waves quilt (figure 38), in black with a little red on white, evokes the atmosphere and era of the Vermont hill farm from which it came. Technological developments, too, had their effect—advances in production efficiency, methods of pattern-printing and dye chemistry bringing cheaper cloth in a greater variety of designs and colors

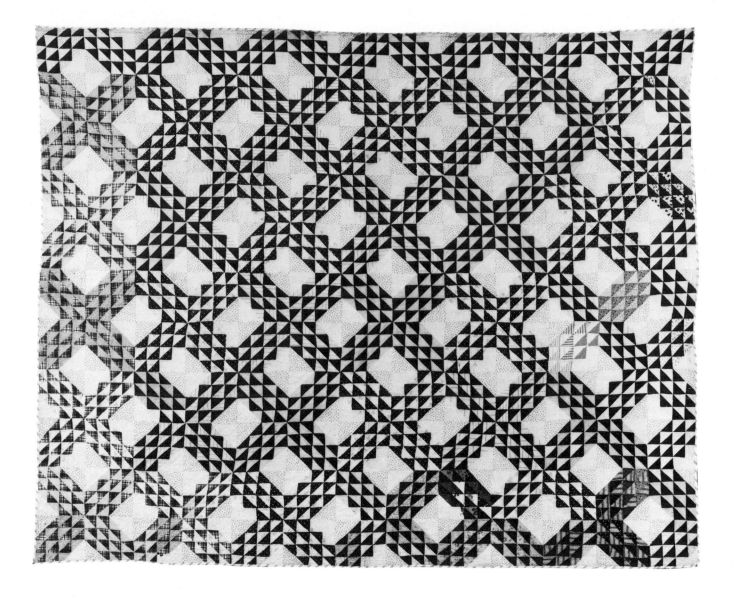

to the American woman, and, ultimately, her quilts. Paralleling this in painting is the exploitation of technological developments, such as the use of plastic paints (with their particular "look" as compared to traditional oil-based paints), and work methods and materials adopted from industrial processes, and graphic techniques borrowed from commercial art.

I discussed earlier the derivation of various types of geometric images found in pieced quilts. In most quilt patterns, any intended image is usually carried in a single block; where the blocks are meant to link, images may appear in the finished quilt only after the blocks are joined (Kaleidoscope, plate 16, Pineapple, plate 60). The process of creating and naming these images is similar to that same process as it operates in the production of "art" objects. In the first type, geometric abstractions drawn directly from nature or man-made objects (Mod-

Figure 38. Ocean Waves. Vermont, c. 1870. 96½″ x 78″. The entire surface is black-on-white with the exception of a few splashes of red which show up here as lighter areas on the left and in a few other spots. The pattern is a successful abstract translation of the movement of the sea. It was made far from the ocean, on a Vermont hill-farm.

ernistic Tulip, plate 64, Schoolhouse, plate 62), the objects are reduced to their basic forms and extraneous decoration is removed; the same general process occurred, say, in the conversion of a bottle into the form it took on a Cubist canvas. The object retains its general characteristics, in an abstracted form, and is immediately recognizable as bottle, house, flower. The quiltmaker, of course, because of the confines of the technique, necessarily geometricized her image, while the painter had greater latitude, and used that formation by choice. The second group includes more generalized images from nature (Wild Goose Chase, plate 63, Ocean Waves, figure 38). These are of a type which are commonly seen in abstract, but not non-objective, painting. Mondrian, for instance, before he turned to a completely non-objective style, painted a series of abstractions which ". . . were based on the sea and the pier at Schevengen as seen from a fourth floor window . . ."; the paintings, dark, monochromatic strokes on a neutral canvas, render the movement of the sea using only short horizontal and vertical lines.[5] There is a very similar solution in the Ocean Waves pattern, figure 38, mostly black materials on a white background with a little use of dull red on each end. Here too, the impression is one of the constant motion and flow of the sea, simply depicted in series of small diamonds. The differences between these first two types of images are the differences between specific and generalized images.

The next type of geometric image, much rarer, is one which, in a "readable" abstract form, expresses events, ideas, and the like; they might be called abstract pictographs (Burgoyne Surrounded, Robbing Peter to Pay Paul, plate 46). Here, it is difficult to tell whether the designs were made in response to the event or idea, or the patterns suggested the subjects after they were made, just as an artist can by intent form and name abstract images which suggest, without literal visual references, complex ideas or events, or he can title his work in response to an idea suggested to him by his forms after the work is completed. This is also true for the fourth type of pieced quilt image, those whose iconographies are not apparent, and whose titles were given them by their inventors to signify the idea or object which prompted them to create that design, or whose title was chosen in response to some inner meaning suggested to the maker by the finished appearance of the form; in neither case will the link be apparent to the onlooker. Some abstract painters, again, follow this method, supplying their paintings with titles for reasons which may or may not be discernible to the viewer.

Artists such as Mondrian eventually succeeded in removing any references to nature in their work, yet succeeded, by the manipulation of simple form and color, in expressing complex emotions and ideas. The discovery by abstract artists that this was indeed possible—that a full range of emotion, meaning, and complex symbolism could be evoked through simple forms, surfaces, and colors with no specific references to nature—was one of the great discoveries of twentieth-century art. Proceeding from a classical philosophical base, a notion of the primacy of basic forms and spatial arrangements, they went on to use the forms in the creation of extremely evocative images. Mondrian wished to express "pure reality in terms of paint." Mondrian felt that "the appearance of natural form changes, but reality remains constant. To create pure reality plastically, it is necessary to reduce natural forms to the constant elements of form and natural colour to primary colour. The aim is not to create other particular forms and colours with their own limitations, but to work towards abolishing them in the interest of a larger unity."[6] Quiltmakers similarly used basic forms and colors to create images which are evocative of complex feelings and associations, as well as those which celebrate simply the beauty of geometric form and strong color.

Color was, of course, co-equal with form in quiltmaking just as it is in painting; in conjunction, they are the quilt or the painting. Quiltmakers took full advantage of the color possibilities they found in their materials, showing a sure grasp of chromatic dynamics. When they wished to emphasize bold form, they would often limit their palette to primary colors, as in the Carpenter's Wheel quilt, plate 22, the Sawtooth or Tree of Life quilt, plate 86, and the Wild Goose Chase, plate 63. Equally they could exploit the most subtle variations of color and pattern in their textiles to create lively (plate 67), romantic (plate 70), or delicate (plate 55) effects. They could blend the most unlikely colors successfully (Robbing Peter to Pay Paul, plate 45, and Melon Patch, plate 46), and could produce an equally moving effect with a minimum of tonality (Log Cabin, plate 49). They understood how to use strong accents to tie together composition; in block-style crazy quilts, such as that shown in plate 25, and in most Log Cabin quilts, such as those in plates 68 and 69 and 44, the block centers on a usually red, sometimes orange, purple, or green square; its purpose is to set a focus for a visually complicated block, composed of many pieces, and to establish a larger unity of such focusing points when the blocks are set together. In the Sawtooth quilt, plate 86, red is used to activate a monochromatic surface; in the Star of Le Moyne quilt, plate 67, the solid red stars in two sizes offer a brilliant counterpoint to the multicolored and complex linked stars. In the Road to California quilt, plate 71, red triangles form an aggressive grid which gives the otherwise recessive pattern dimensionality.

They could exploit the color and form of natural phenomena, as in the Rainbow quilt, plate 21, where that event has been translated in a linear fashion into patterns of great force and intensity. In such designs as Baby Blocks (plates 50 and 52), they created projective optical-illusion patterns by manipulating color and form in a relatively simple manner. In the architecturally rendered quilt, plate 73, its complex effect built from only two elements, squares and trapezoids, interior space is opened, the effect aided by the ingenious device of adding a line of fancy stitching in a contrasting color along the upward-slanting edge of each square's right-hand upright; this tends to connect each upright to its proper components and leads the eye into the center, creating the optical effect.

They could use strong strokes of color in an expressionistic manner (crazy quilt, plate 26), and even "paint" representational scenes with small blocks of color (plate 66). Here, the maker depicted clouds, light through the tree, tree bark, flowers before the house (with blocks of striped material), and suggested interior space.

Color, like basic forms, has emotional weight. Gropius felt: "Forms and colours gain meaning only in so far as they are related to our inner selves. . . . Red, for instance, evokes in us other emotions than does blue or yellow, round forms speak differently to us than do pointed or jagged ones. The elements which constitute the grammar of creation are its rules of rhythm, of proportion, of light values, of full or empty space." Quiltmakers were acutely aware of the symbolic possibilities of color, as shown in those quilts which embody references to nature: the Feathered Star quilt, plate 75, in the fire-colors of red, yellow, and white, set against dark blue, catches the blazing of stars in the firmament; the Birds-in-the-Air quilt, plate 76, successfully evokes the swift movement of birds in sunlight. They were equally capable of chromatic manipulations for more general emotive effects, as in the Around-the-World quilt, plate 55, in which the soft colors and fine patterns work together to destroy the boundaries of the blocks.

Many of the patterns have an overt symbolism which was clear to both the makers and the viewers of the quilts. Some patterns, such as WCTU (for Women's Christian Temperance Union) which is always made in the blue and white colors of that organization, had the obvious intent of showing that household's adherence to the principles of alcoholic abstention. Such patterns as Underground Railroad, Whig's Defeat, and Fifty-Four-Forty-or-Fight similarly reflected abolitionist, political, and national sympathies. There were reminders of the proper religious life in Pilgrim's Progress and Heavenly Steps, or the vagaries, pains, ecstasies, and mysteries of life in Wheel of Fortune, Wandering Foot, Widow's Troubles, True Lover's Knot, Prosperity Block, Star of Hope, Young Man's Fancy, and Ship of Dreams.

Choosing the basic pattern was the simplest step in a creative process which ended in the finished quilt. There were conscious aesthetic decisions to be made all along, each affecting the final result. Many of these decisions were made in conjunction with practical considerations: How big must the quilt be to fit the bed? What materials were available? Was there time to make an intricate quilt, and was that desired, or was this to be a simple pattern, quickly made to answer a pressing need? Was there enough of a certain color to answer the requirements of a particular design? Such decisions as these would then be made: How big should the blocks be? Should there be a border, or borders, and how should the blocks be set apart if such a pattern was contemplated? What colors should be used in each part of the block, the borders, the separating strips? Did an existing design answer the maker's aesthetic desires, or should she vary it, or design a new one? If there is not enough of one color, what could be substituted which would not disrupt the overall harmony and plan? There were infinite choices to be made. While the established format for each design might seem limiting, it is obvious that this was not the case; rather, the block-style furnished a work method and a geometrically based aesthetic which was endlessly variable and could be manipulated for the most diverse results. No two quilts are ever alike, though they often share the same pattern; an examination of the many Log Cabin quilts in the plates will show how different sensibilities applied to the same basic design produced totally different results.

Many writers on the subject have said incorrectly, I think, that the confining nature of set pieced quilt patterns limited the quiltmaker's art, while the appliqué quilt, in which cloth can be cut to any design which occurs to the craftsman, is actually the form in which greater creativity can be shown. In the United States, as I have mentioned, appliqué and pieced work appear in combination in quilts of the late eighteenth century. Pure appliqué quilts reached their peak in mid-nineteenth century, slightly before what I think is the great era of pieced work. They became the "elegant" quilts, upon which extra care and time, the best materials, and most intricate quilting were lavished. Designs were drawn largely from nature, flowers, trees, figures; such motifs were rendered either quite realistically or with some measure of abstraction and simplification, the latter style predominating. It is my opinion that this developed from the broderie perse quilts of the late eighteenth and early nineteenth centuries, in which natural forms cut from textiles printed with figurative designs were applied to a white ground. These quilts were considered very elegant, and were a showcase for needlework prowess, due to the fine stitchery which was required to sew down these intricate figures without causing the edges to pucker. Those who had no

Figure 39. Lobster. New York, c. 1860. 75″ x 75″. An appliqué idea similar to that in figure 25, but here the block-style is more emphatically a part of the overall design. The basic design is one of stylized flowers.

access to the expensive chintzes from which broderie perse figures were cut could have copied the style, drawing their own figures and using the solid and patterned textiles available to them. Naturally, designs would be simplified to an outline form; the quilters did not have the ability in draftsmanship to draw the realistic figures, which would in any case have been meaningless without the fine internal details which skilled textile painters and printers gave their realistic forms. The American predilection for simplifying forms was no doubt also at work. Broderie perse quilts ran strongly to floral cut-outs, and so do appliqué quilts. They were done in a number of styles: block-style with repeated motifs (figure 39); block-style with a different design in each block, as in Baltimore or Album quilts (figure 40—these quilts tend to have very realistic designs); there are large, balanced overall designs which are assembled directly on the full quilt top (figure 12); and rare "scenes" (landscapes or events) depicted either quite

Figure 40. Appliqué quilt, Album style. Dated 1857. Inscribed "Anna Putney Farrington." 100" x 98". A fine Album quilt, each block different. This style is often associated with quilts of the Baltimore region. The designs are often highly realistic, and are the ultimate examples of this trend in quilt appliqué. (Collection of Cora Ginsburg)

realistically or in a manner akin to "naive" painting. And there are minor variations on all of these styles.

It is my feeling that appliqué quilts generally show less variety, invention, and ingenuity than pieced quilts; the designs are often more static, colors more limited. An enormous number are done in aniline reds and greens only, and are of the period when materials dyed with those colors were first introduced, indicating their makers' concern with fashion. For the quiltmaker, the pieced block dictated the use of basic geometric forms, the possibilities of which were later sensed and exploited by abstract painters. I do not mean to imply that appliqué quilts are not beautiful, for many certainly are; but their beauty is more of a decorative nature than that seen in the best of the pieced quilts, which when successful are the results of legitimate aesthetic questions having been posed and most convincingly resolved. The license to draw freely, if it is encumbered with considerations of what is "elegant" or in "good taste," may be more confining than finding creative solutions within a given format. This was successfully demonstrated by Albers and other painters. Alan Solomon, writing of Noland's circle paintings, said: "The circle motifs, then, provide an absolute, rigidly disciplined scheme which emphasizes all the more the spirit of free inventive play which underlies their manipulation so that Noland's solutions, from painting to painting, are always surprising and fresh. At the same time, each painting implies a struggle against easy resolution of the tonal, textural and spatial situation; this in part explains the ability of the image to renew itself constantly in his work."[7] The statement implies the artist's awareness of an intellectual process behind his painting; while, as I have noted, the same cannot be claimed for quiltmakers, it is certain that their manipulations of form and color involved the same sort of freedom of imagination working through an established system. My choice is a personal, aesthetic one: I prefer the extraordinary invention and tough visual qualities of great pieced quilts to what are to my eye the more decorative characteristics of most appliqué quilts.

Visually, not all pieced quilts are great or even good. Many are mediocre or uninteresting, an equal number are competent and pleasing, again, decorative; these two categories make up the great majority. It is the exceptional ones, made by women of superior eyes, hands, and sensibilities, which stand as important visual statements. While many women in a given town or area might share the same designs and buy the same materials at the local store which served them all, their results were, of course, totally different, reflecting their varying tastes and abilities. And there was no assurance that more than one woman of the area, if even one, would produce great quilts. A woman with confidence in her aesthetic decisions would develop a distinct style which marked her quilts, much as an artist develops a style which is distinctly his own.

It is unusual to find a number of quilts together made by the same woman once a century or more has gone by, since they are usually widely scattered after several generations, especially if they were the products of a skilled maker whose productions were prized. When it does occur, however, the quilts are usually consistent in style. The three quilts in plates 79, 80, and 81 were made by a Pennsylvania woman in the last half of the nineteenth century. All show a fondness for unusual "crazy" centers in block designs, the first two of which are of her own invention, the last a Spider Web pattern with a crazy center substituted for the normal two-color, regularly patterned mid-part (see the Spider's Web quilt, plate 82). She separated her blocks widely, and used strongly patterned materials for her dividing strips and borders. There is a good deal of movement in her designs, in part a result of her sparing but skillful use of reds to enliven her surfaces.

There were occasional cohesive and contained groups of people whose work was uniformly excellent. I think particularly of the Amish, very few of whose pieced quilts of the types peculiar to them are anything but visually interesting and exciting. The Amish have continued to hold off outside influences to a remarkable degree, and many of the quilts they still make in the traditional style retain the feeling of the older ones in design and color even though they employ modern materials.

It is ironic that pieced quilt design of what I consider to be the best sort grew and reached its height as the excesses of Victorian design became pervasive. One is tempted to see in that a reaction of country women against those extravagances of fashion, taste, dress, design, and decorum intruding on a milieu which had been for several centuries characterized by the products of functional design and informed by the ideals of simplicity in manner. But the idea would be difficult to support, and it is likely that the tradition of geometrically oriented pieced quiltmaking, which itself developed so that there was in the end as much virtue and acclaim in an extremely complicated, beautifully crafted example as in a fine appliqué quilt, had created a momentum which carried it with little harm to its basic soundness through the Victorian period. Quilts quite in keeping with Victorian design sensibilities were made during that long era, but they neither supplanted the growth nor impeded the flowering of the pieced quilt tradition.

It is remarkable that that tradition, under the pressures of contemporary life and the availability of the products of industrialization, which have curtailed most handcrafts, has not ended. The craft is still practiced as it always was, though now more for relaxation than out of necessity, and to answer a demand for things which smack more of the hand than the machine. Some have taken up the craft and follow it in its conventional form for leisure-time amusement or because it represents a tradition they find emotionally significant. Others have found in quiltmaking a medium which they can manipulate to their aesthetic ends and have evolved new styles and techniques. The feeling of contemporary culture and the conclusions of its art are beginning to appear in their quilts. Perhaps the technique will become, now that its products are no longer functionally necessary, one of a number in the spectrum of creative forms, but one which uniquely couples the tactile and special color possibilities of materials and dimensionality with the ability to handle the classic artistic concerns of line, form, color.

Concurrently, and especially in the rural areas of America, women continue to make pieced quilts because they always have done so, because it is still a skill which is honored. The patterns which originated centuries ago are still used, and new ones are constantly invented. Where taste and self-consciousness do not interfere, as they often do among those who take up quilting because needlework is fashionable, pieced quilts continue to reflect their times and changing fashion as accurately and eloquently as they did centuries ago. The lively quilt in plate 85 catches the flavor of contemporary America: plastic colors, both hot and cool, chosen not as a comment but because they came from those materials available at local stores, and which the maker and her contemporaries use for clothes and furnishings. While it might now appear less elegantly realized than many of the quilts illustrated, it is evocative of its time and similarly moving.

It would be encouraging to think that American women would thus continue the tradition begun by their sisters over three centuries ago. Necessity demanded of them the production of warm bedcovers for their families. They responded over the years with the creation of a distinctive body of work which combines functional efficiency with sometimes extraordinary beauty. Pieced quiltmaking was an ingenious compromise with necessity, in which a problem—how to assemble a needed utilitarian object from available materials—was the impetus for a solution at once functional and aesthetically important. The best of their designs, based on those fundamental geometric forms which are agelessly beautiful, have that vitality, freshness, and validity which are the moving qualities of distinguished visual objects of any type, and of any place or time.

Figure 41. Harvest Sun, c. 1930. 84½″ x 73½″. An Art Deco fan quilt, the fans becoming rising suns. While the surface appears jumbled at first, there is a regular pattern of round-ended crosses.

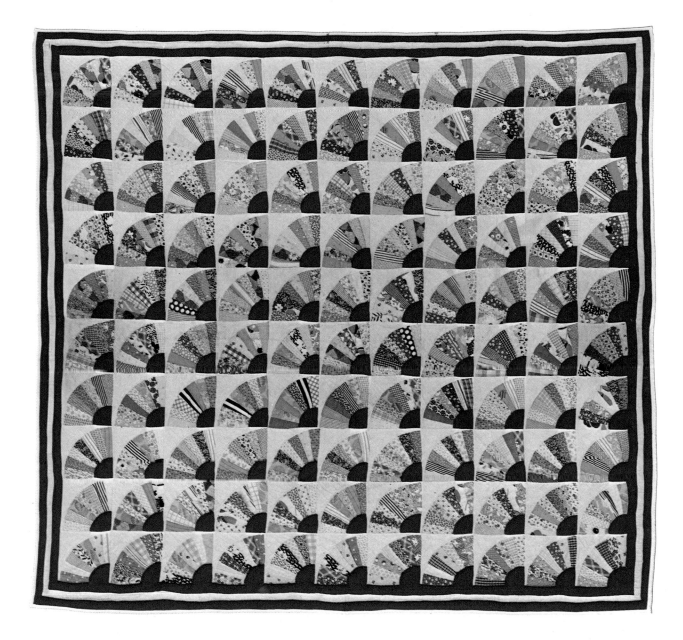

Plate 47. Fannie's Fan. Pennsylvania, c. 1935. Cotton. 76″ x 71″. An Art Deco fan, here showing the Oriental influence on the style. Compare with plate 48 and figure 41.

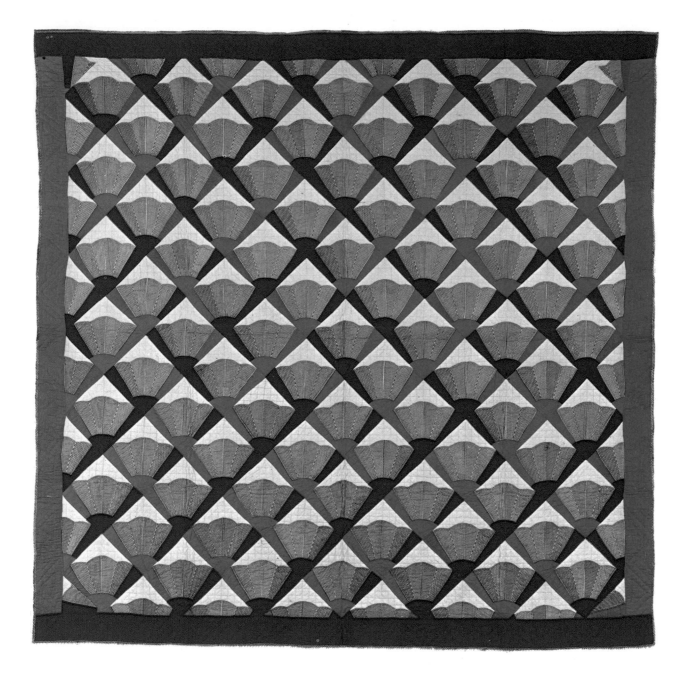

Plate 48. Art Deco Fans. New York, c. 1930. Cotton. 82″ x 82″. Pure Art Deco design, using striped materials and stylized fan motifs, an indication that the design trends of any era can be assimilated successfully into pieced quilt design.

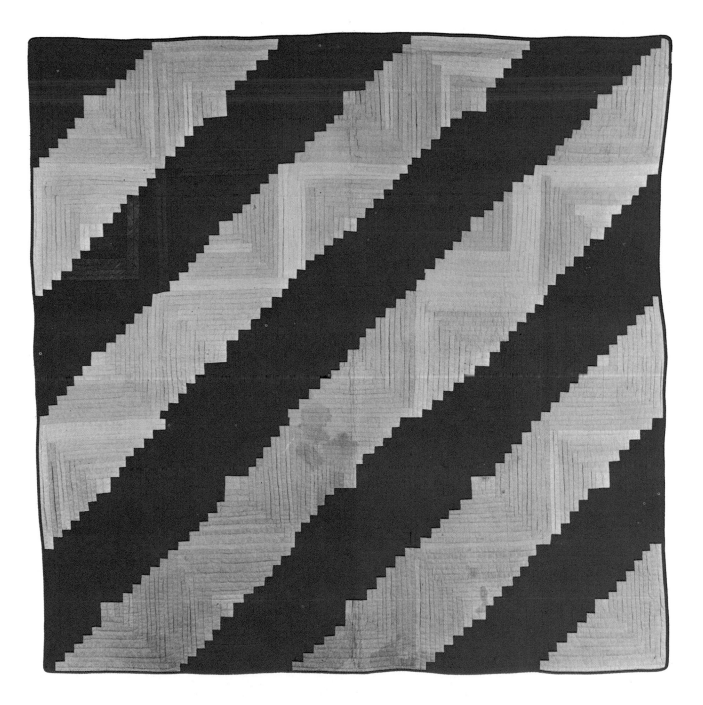

Plate 49. Log Cabin—Straight Furrow. Pennsylvania, c. 1860. Cotton. 74″ x 74″. An
unusual Log Cabin block, here without the usual strong center square in the common
red or yellow, perhaps so constructed because there is no pattern in the materials
used and thus no need for a central focusing point. While the stripes forming the blue
and red parts of the blocks are of similar tonalities, they are actually the leftover scraps
from many different shirts and dresses.

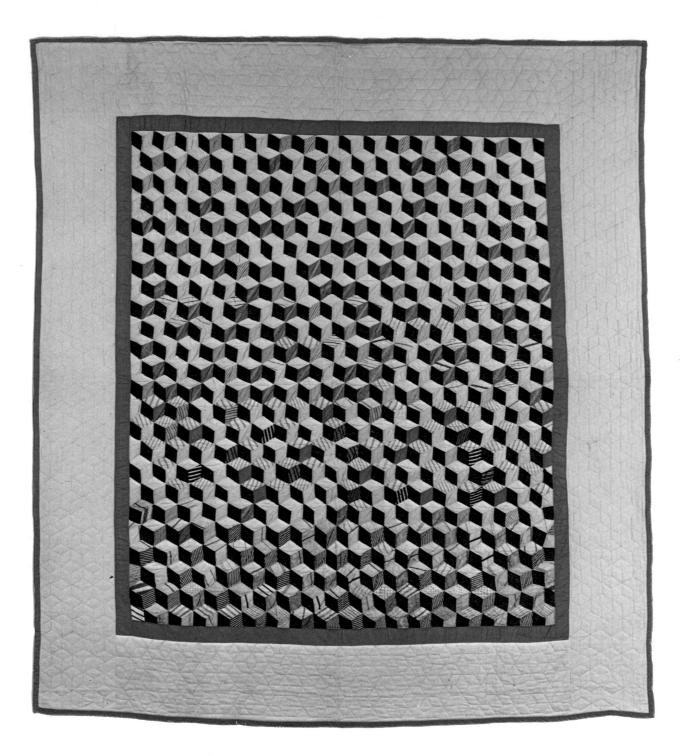

Plate 50. Baby Blocks, Cube Illusion, or Pandora's Box. Pennsylvania, 1875. Cotton.
73″ x 73″. Most of the materials in the blocks are from men's shirts. The muted color
scheme and intricate ''draftsmanship'' give the quilt a drawing-like quality, all neatly
compressed within a frame.

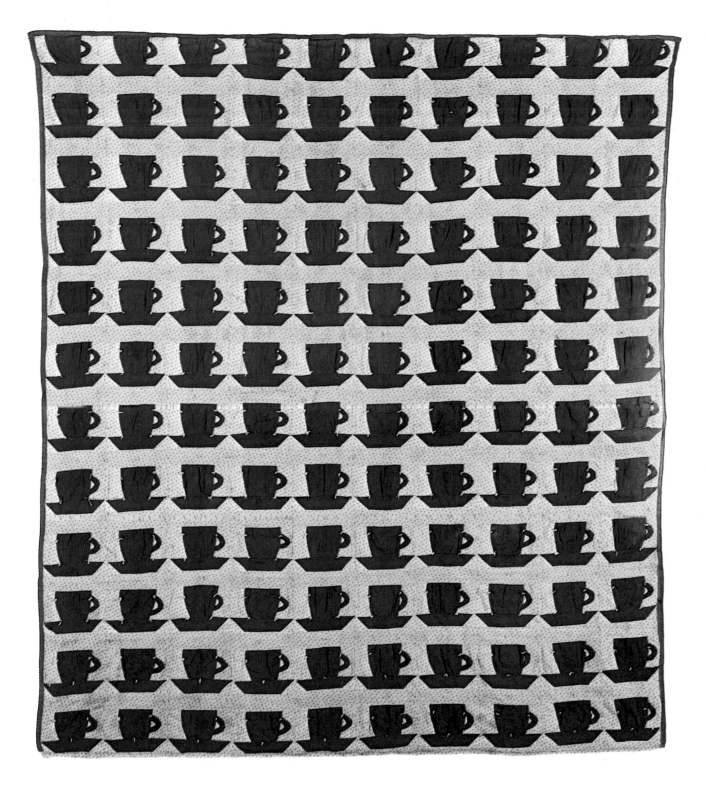

Plate 51. Coffee Cups. Colorado, c. 1910. Cotton. 80½″ x 69″. Such direct
abstractions of the basic forms of common objects are quite unusual; this of a cup
and saucer is unique, the more common images are the Basket and Schoolhouse. The
repetitive image in a two-color format is graphically very effective; its graphic
sophistication makes it difficult to envision this as a bedcover.

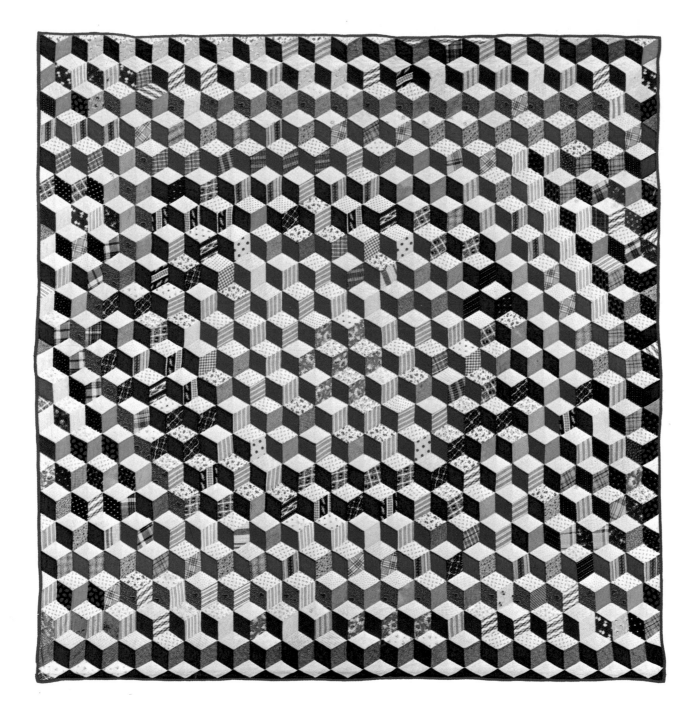

Plate 53. Detail of plate 52.

Plate 52 (left). Baby Blocks, Cube Illusion, or Pandora's Box.
Pennsylvania, c. 1880. Cotton. 83½″ x 81″. The use of this
pattern which originated in the last half of the nineteenth
century is similar to the optical experiments of some
contemporary painters.

Plate 54. Detail of plate 81.

Plate 55 (left). Around the World. New Hampshire, c. 1935. Cotton. 101½″ x 79″. A subdued quilt from the Depression years, showing the signs of much use and laundering. The design is most delicately edged in the patterns of the cheap cottons.

Plate 56. Detail of plate 55.

Plate 57. Triple Irish Chain. Pennsylvania, c. 1870. Wool and cotton. 78″ x 75″. The potential interplay of the reflective qualities of different materials—here the figured cottons of the small squares and the wools of the solid red blocks—was exploited occasionally by quiltmakers. In general, cottons are ''brighter'' and advance visually more than wools.

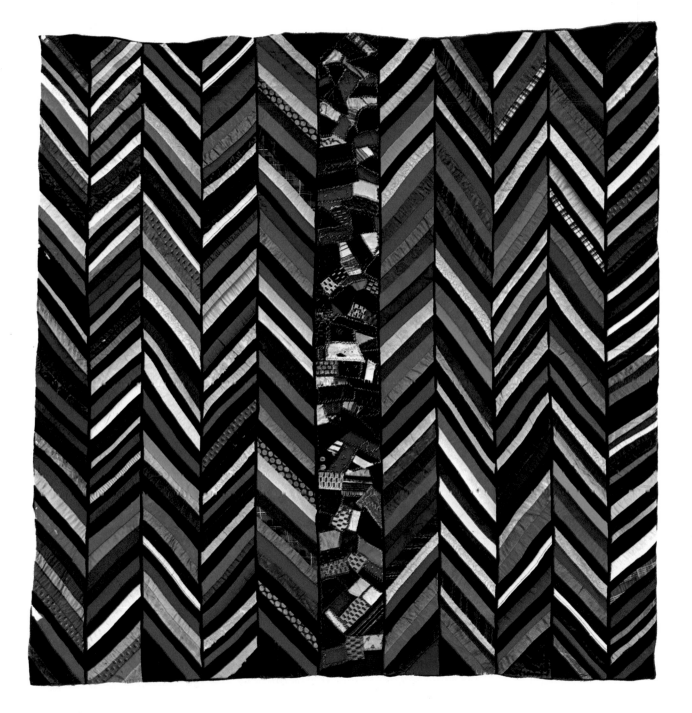

Plate 58. Diagonal Stripes with crazy center panel. Pennsylvania, c. 1875. Silk and velvet. 78″ x 75″. This quilt is a showcase of the rich silks and velvets beloved in its era. The central crazy strip is an area of flat chaos compressed and held in check by the columns of chevrons.

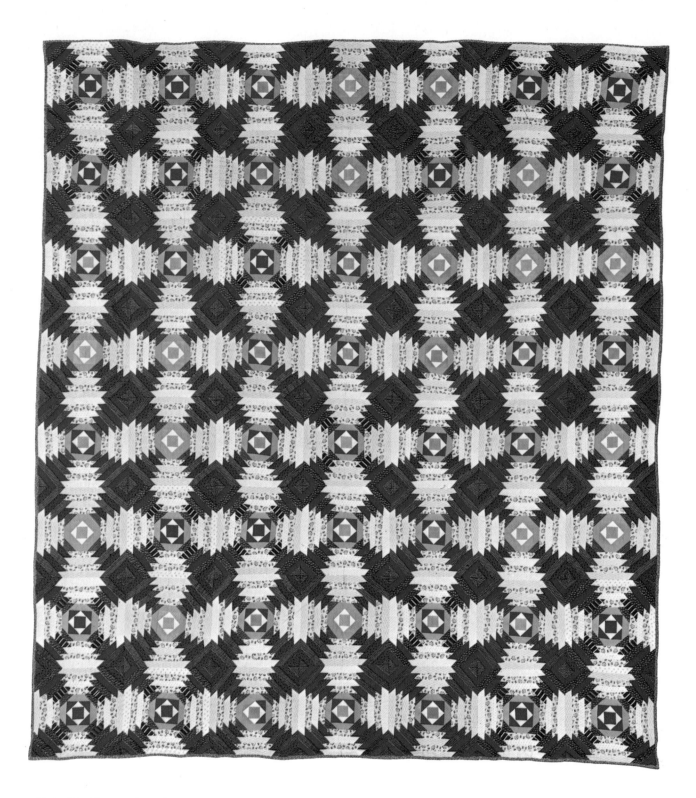

Plate 59. Pineapples. New Jersey, c. 1875. Cotton. 92″ x 87″. Pineapples were a beloved symbol of hospitality in Colonial America, often appearing on the posts of entrance gateways. The calm square and diamond centers save the lively surface from incoherence. The pattern is also called Maltese Cross.

Plate 60. Detail of plate 59.

Plate 61. Sawtooth. Pennsylvania, c. 1880. Cotton. 84″ x 84″. A favorite Pennsylvania form—bold central diamond in a square—here with a Sawtooth edge. This pattern is difficult to resolve at corners, and the maker of this quilt had several different solutions.

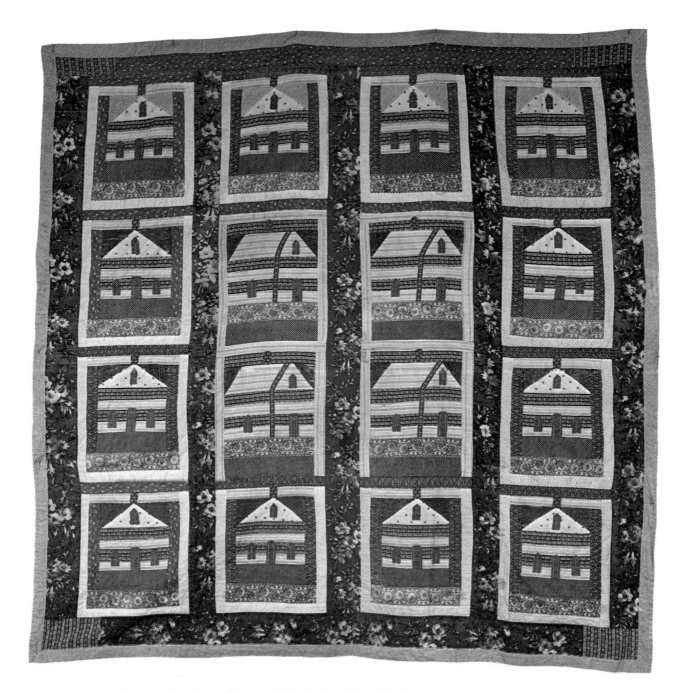

Plate 62. Schoolhouse. New Hampshire, c. 1880. Cotton. 77″ x 76″. An early and unusual interpretation of this idea, showing two views of the subject; the side view alone is the common block (figure 2).

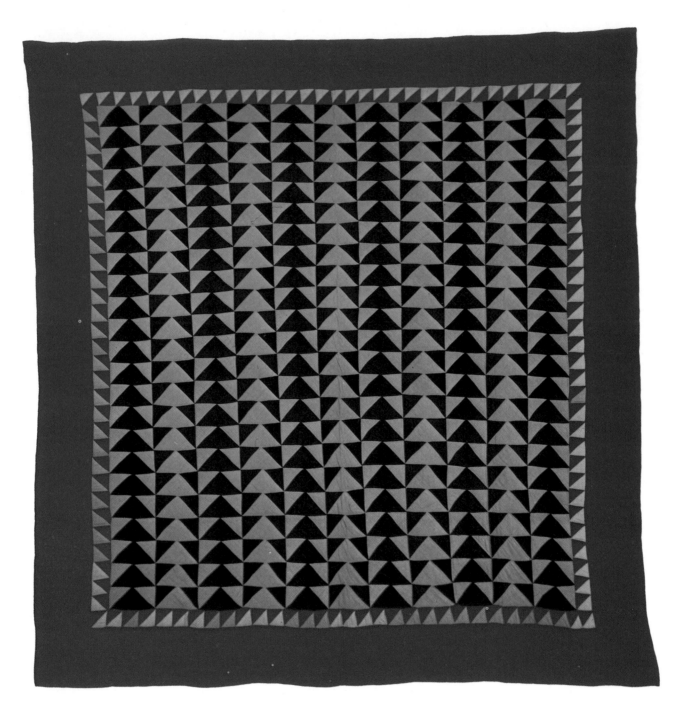

Plate 63. Wild Goose Chase. Pennsylvania, c. 1910. Cotton. 88" x 81". The pattern
in a pure form—and very optical. Pennsylvanians often used bold primary colors in
simple patterns for such effects.

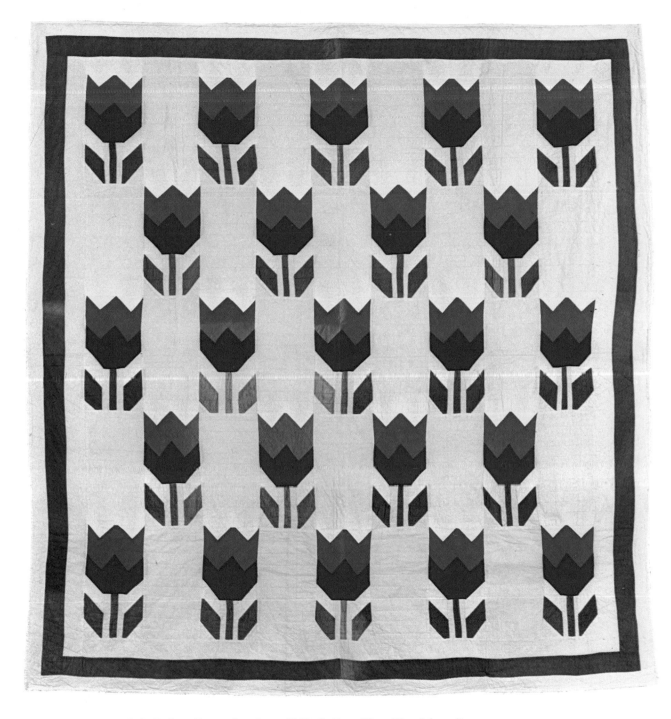

Plate 64. Modernistic Tulips. Pennsylvania, c. 1910. Cotton. 82″ x 76″. A favorite
motif of the Pennsylvania craftsman in one of its many manifestations; here, a stylized
abstraction done in shapes suitable for a straight-cut pieced block.

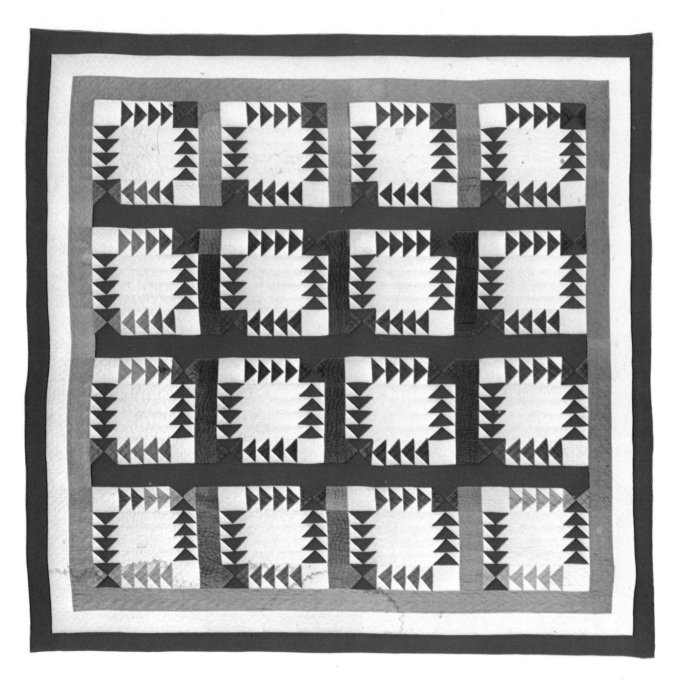

Plate 65 (above). Wild Goose Chase. Pennsylvania, c. 1870. Cotton. 83″ x 83″. A unique variation of the Wild Goose Chase motif. The greens, typically, have faded, while the reds have remained vivid, a common result from what were the new aniline dyes shortly after mid-nineteenth century.

Plate 66 (right). House in the Country. New England, c. 1870. Cotton. 75″ x 57½″. Such representational scenes, especially in pieced work, are extremely rare. Objects, light, interior space, perspective were rendered using small squares and the colors and patterns of the maker's materials.

Plate 67. Star of Le Moyne. New England, c. 1850. Cotton chintz. 87″ x 74″. A great pieced quilt, stars within stars within the spaces formed by stars. A dazzling, unique, and highly successful overall pattern. (America Hurrah Antiques, N.Y.C.)

Plate 68. Log Cabin—Barn Raising. Pennsylvania, c. 1880. Cotton. 86″ x 80″. A
clean-lined Barn Raising formed by blocks using bright materials with little pattern.
It is quite different from the quilt in plate 69.

Plate 69. Log Cabin—Barn Raising. New Jersey, c. 1920. Cotton top. 88″ x 70″. The profusion of figured materials creates a frenetic surface barely laced together by the solid bright centers of the blocks.

Plate 70. Fence Posts. Pennsylvania, c. 1935. Cotton. 74" x 69". A Depression-era quilt in typically subdued colors. The concentration of greens in the center holds the pattern together; it has a very romantic, landscape-like quality.

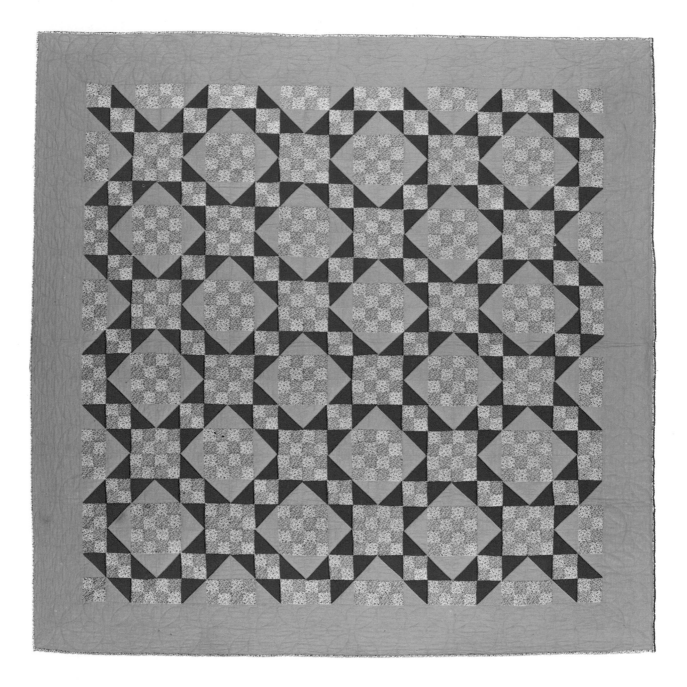

Plate 71. Road to California. Pennsylvania, c. 1900. Cotton. 78″ x 78″. Plastic colors
pre-plastics. The reds activate an otherwise static surface.

Plate 72. Detail of plate 71.

Plate 73 (left). Attic Windows. New Hampshire, c. 1910. Wool. 62″ x 49″. A complex-appearing design which is actually formed by only two elements: a black square and a trapezoid. The illusion of inner space it creates is aided by a line of fancy stitching that runs along the slanting edge of each upright. (Collection of Blanche Greenstein and Tom Woodard)

Plate 74 (above). Crazy. New England, c. 1920. Cotton. 88″ x 84″. Futuristic design in a crazy-style quilt.

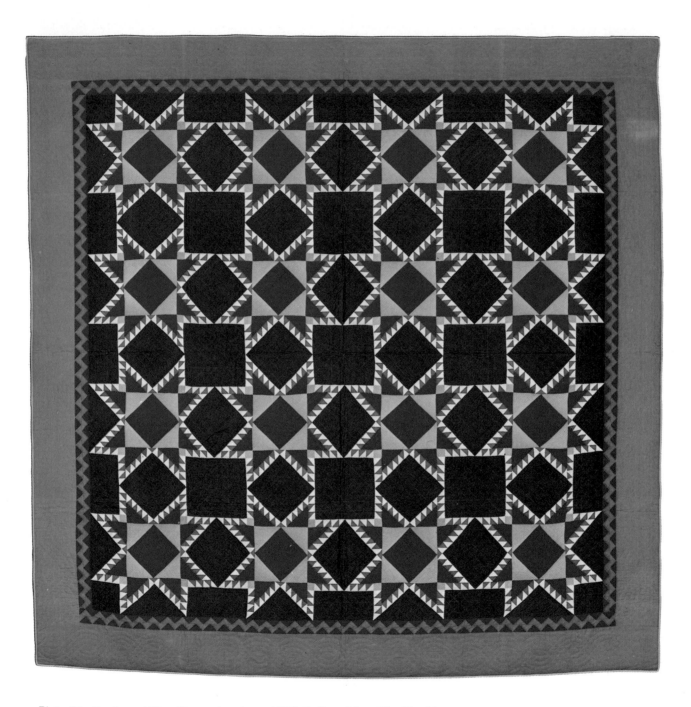

Plate 75. Feathered Star. Pennsylvania, c. 1890. Cotton. 80″ x 80″. The blue squares and diamonds opened in the design can advance visually to form large blazing figures themselves, or break down into separate elements which retreat behind the feathered stars. (Collection of Bill Gallick and Tony Ellis)

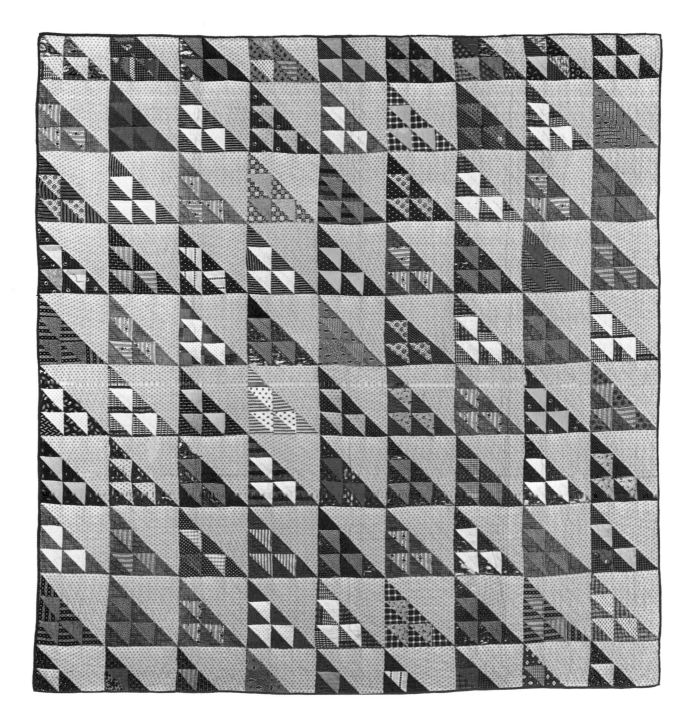

Plate 76. Birds in the Air. Pennsylvania, c. 1860. Cotton. 70½″ x 66½″. The lively optical effects and highly stylized avian forms successfully evoke the image of swift birds moving in the sunlight.

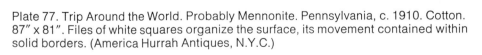

Plate 77. Trip Around the World. Probably Mennonite. Pennsylvania, c. 1910. Cotton. 87″ x 81″. Files of white squares organize the surface, its movement contained within solid borders. (America Hurrah Antiques, N.Y.C.)

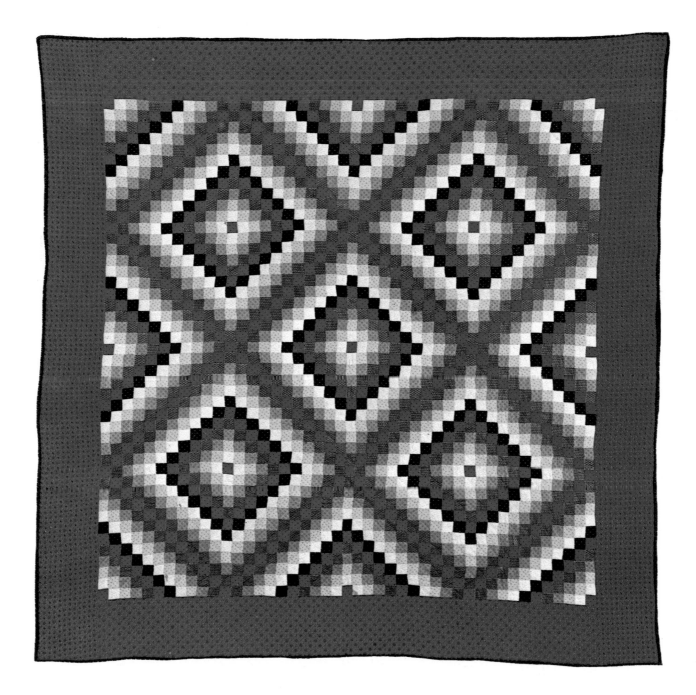

Plate 78. Trip Around the World. Mennonite. Pennsylvania, c. 1910. Cotton. 85″ x 85″.
A relatively simple but potentially extremely effective pattern if, as here, the colors
are carefully chosen.

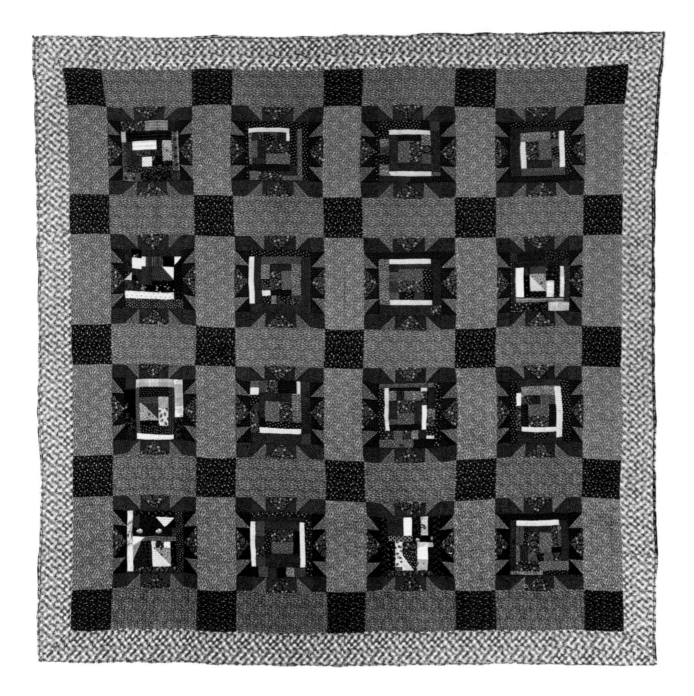

Plate 79. Crazy—Stars. Pennsylvania, c. 1870. Cotton. 82" x 81". This and the next two quilts, plates 80 and 81, are the work of one woman whose taste ran to "crazy" centers in her blocks and boldly patterned materials for borders and sashes.

Plate 80. Crazy—Blocks. Pennsylvania, c. 1875. Cotton. 89″ x 82″. A simple but effective block of the maker's invention. The use of red in the block centers and a thin border effectively tie the design together.

Plate 81. Spider Web. Pennsylvania, c. 1890. Cotton. 80" x 80". A unique variation
of the Spider Web pattern in keeping with this maker's fondness for blocks with
"crazy" elements. The pink spans between the star's points—in contrast with the
surrounding red—effectively suggest the gossamer of a web. (See detail, plate 54.)

Plate 82. Spider Web. Pennsylvania, c. 1885. Cotton. 81½″ x 81½″. Here the Spider
Web block, in contrast to its use in plate 81, is employed without borders, and thus
forms additional large patterns in the overall design. The little yellow Maltese crosses,
formed where the points of the stars meet, have an insect-like appearance.

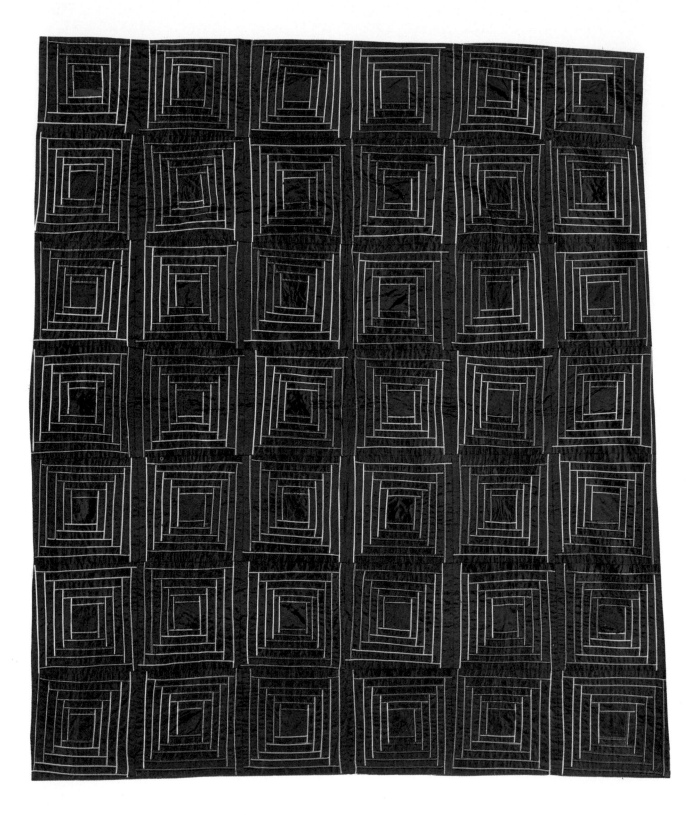

Plate 83. Log Cabin—Courthouse Steps. Connecticut, c. 1910. Silk. 76″ x 73″. The Log Cabin block in a unique variant, the lines of the pattern formed by the colored selvedges of dark silk ribbons.

Plate 84. Fly Foot or Catch Me if You Can—among many names for this pattern.
Pennsylvania, c. 1900. Cotton. 66″ x 64″. A nice juggling of subdued materials. The
four blocks in the interstices of the main X-form reverse the normal block pattern,
giving the design an added lightness.

Plate 85. Field of Diamonds or Rainbow Tile. Nebraska, 1972. Cotton. 92″ x 80″. The stuff of American homemade clothing, 1972. These colors and patterns are those of good but inexpensive cottons widely sold throughout the country, and used in family clothesmaking. They are the colors of contemporary America.

Plate 86. Sawtooth. Massachusetts, c. 1875. Cotton. 88½″ x 77½″. Red and white in an expansive, bold image. All such Sawtooth edges are pieced in strips, in alternating triangles of each color.

Plate 87 (above). Star of Bethlehem. Pennsylvania, c. 1880. Cotton. 85½″ x 82″. Pennsylvania exuberance in a favorite pattern. The design has the explosive graphic quality of some Pop Art images.

Plate 88 (right). Nebraska, c. 1960. Cotton. Cottons of recent vintage whose strong patterns cause what would otherwise be a very regular surface to break up visually.

Plate 89. Flower Basket. Pennsylvania, c. 1865. Cotton. Another interpretation of the popular Basket block, in a color scheme typical of Pennsylvania work.

Plate 90. Nine-Patch—Barn Raising. Pennsylvania, c. 1885. Cotton. 87″ x 87″. An ingenious variation of the basic Nine-Patch block, here with each square split into half light and dark elements, and the blocks arranged to form radiating light and dark diamonds. The orange diamond within a solid red square, in turn within a solid blue diamond, gives a coherent central focusing point. (Rhea Goodman, Quilt Gallery, Inc.)

Plate 91. Log Cabin—W. Pennsylvania, c. 1875. Cotton. 82″ x 82″. An unusual use
of the Log Cabin form in an overall pattern, demonstrating the versatility of such
half-light and half-dark blocks. The deep saturated colors set against pale yellows,
pinks, and whites and the large gestures of the design make for a very lively surface.
(Collection of Bill Gallick and Tony Ellis)

Plate 92. T's. New York, c. 1910. Cotton. 86″ x 80″. Red, white, and blue in idiosyncratic images, two lines of which suggest an abstract pictographic writing system. Such manipulations of form indicate the most conscious ''painterly'' intentions on the part of quiltmakers. (America Hurrah Antiques, N.Y.C.)

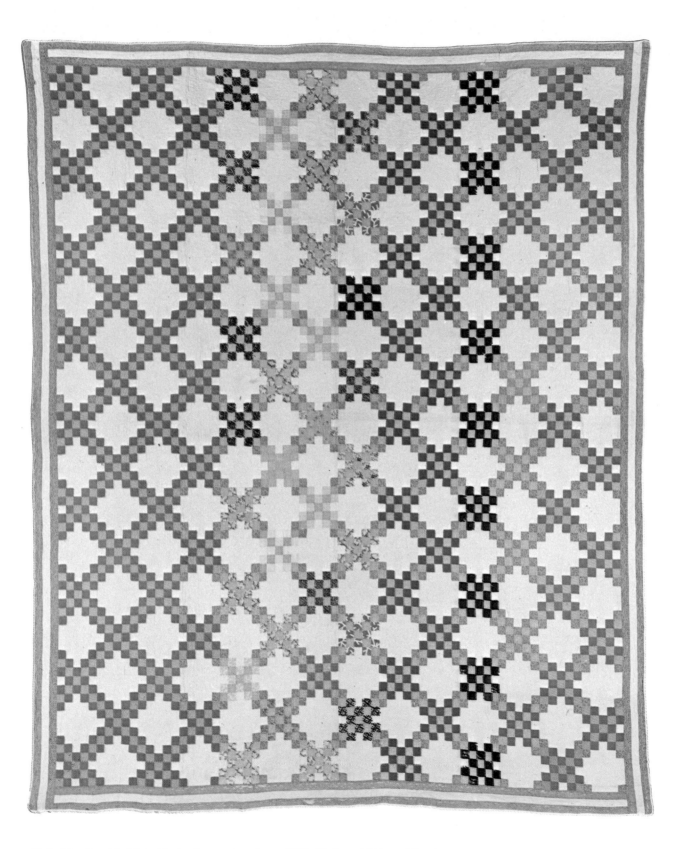

Plate 93. Double Irish Chain. Pennsylvania, c. 1850. Cotton. 93½″ x 78″. A
light-handed exploitation of the color variations in materials; groups of squares with
lighter hues have been assembled to form a long stripe, balanced by a line of dark
blues and a counterpoise of three groups of reds.

Plate 94. Album quilt. New Jersey, c. 1940. Cotton. A typical Album quilt,
the ideal being to have a different design for every block.

Plate 95. Checkerboard. Pennsylvania, c. 1885. Cotton. 75″ x 75″. I believe this—and similar elaborations of the ancient Irish Chain design—was influenced by the adoption in the Victorian era of Near Eastern mosaic design patterns. While they can often be fussy in a small section, American quiltmakers used them successfully in a large format. (Collection of Bill Gallick and Tony Ellis.)

Figure 42. Irish Chain. Pennsylvania, c. 1880. Cotton. 80″ x 79″. The Irish Chain design elaborated, the little squares increased in number so that they form a dominant cross image, reducing the normal preponderance of open space to four areas in the design. (See plate 93 for comparison.) (Collection of Sarah Melvin)

Appendix

"THE CASE OF THE QUILT-MAKERS"

"The Case of the Quilt-Makers" is an interesting document, logically relating to that act of 1720 which outlawed the sale of printed cottons, even those made in England. It is a broadside printed by a group of entrepreneurs who were making quilts for domestic sale in England. They imported white cotton from India to be printed in England, most likely in imitation of Indian "carpets" (this term was used to denote both furniture coverings and coverings for beds). They then bought English wool, Kidderminster, a name usually associated with carpeting, or Kendal, to be used for the back, and wool too short for spinning for the stuffing. The document implies that the actual assembling was done on a piece basis.

The broadside contains a number of most interesting bits of information. If we divide the yardage for the backs (184,000 yards) by the number of "Carpets" printed for making into quilts (23,000), we come up with 8 feet, which must have been about the length of a common English quilt of the period.

It also reveals something about the state of the English cotton printing industry, one which began to use the methods learned from India in the last years of the seventeenth century. The English could not yet spin and weave cotton of sufficient quality for the mordant-dyeing process, so of necessity imported the cotton from India unpainted and unprinted to dye themselves.

The type of quilt the "Quilt-Makers" were producing—cotton top and wool back—is also quite unusual; I know of no examples in this country and I do not think there are any in England. I assume it was for these entrepreneurs the most expedient combination, cheaper English wools with the tops necessarily made of imported cotton, so that they might be printed in imitation of what were undoubtedly the more expensive imported Indian all-cotton quilts.

If we take their figure of 23,000 "Carpets" printed for quilts in a year, and assume that this business might have gone on even ten years, we get the rather amazing total of over 200,000 quilts made for sale by this one group. That is, I feel, a conservative estimate. Not one of these distinctive quilts has ever surfaced. If we speculate that, given this volume of business, there was a popular acceptance and use of such "everyday" quilts, and add the number which must have been made in the home and by other professional groups, and those imported, the probable number of quilts in use during the period is staggering. Yet only a handful is left.

THE
CASE

OF THE

Quilt-Makers,

Sheweth,

HAT the Depriving the Quilt-Makers of the Liberty of Selling Printed Callicoe Carpets, will be a Detriment to the Government and the Woollen Manufacture; as appears from these following Reasons, *Viz.*

There are about 23000 Callicoe Carpets printed in Form *per Ann.* containing 184000 Yards, which Carpets must consequently consume 184000 Yards of *Kidderminster* or *Kendall* Stuffs, of our own Manufacture, us'd for the wrong Sides of Quilts, and 138000 Pound of ordinary Wool, which must otherwise be thrown away, being too short for Spinning, and fit for no other Use.

The Duty on Printing the same Callicoe Carpets amounts to 4600 *l.* per *Annum*, besides the Duty paid by the *East-India* Company on the white Cloth at Importation; and these Carpets are never exported, as Callicoes printed for Garments, which are ship'd off daily, and have a considerable Drawback.

It is therefore humbly hoped, That the Honourable the Commons of *Great Britain* in Parliament Assembled will be pleased to grant a Clause in the Bill now depending in this Honourable House, to permit the Use of printed Callicoe Carpets; it being altogether impracticable to make them into Garments, or any other Houshold Furniture than Quilts, being printed in Form for that Use only; and it is plain, no printed Linen or Stuffs of our own Manufacture are so proper as Callicoe Carpets aforesaid, being lighter and warmer than any other Commodity to be manufactured in that Way. Besides, the taking away that Branch of Trade, will be the Destruction of Abundance of poor Families, that get a comfortable Livelihood by making the said Quilts.

Our Hardship will be greater than any other Dealers in Callicoe, by Reason the Duties we have paid for Printing the Callicoe Carpets now in our Hands, amount to several Thousand Pounds, (and are fit for no other Country, or Use, but the Quilts to which they are apply'd) our Stocks being larger than they would otherwise have been, if the People had not been made apprehensive that they should not quietly enjoy them. So that the Prohibiting the Sale of the same will be the inevitable Ruine of us and our Families, unless a Clause as aforesaid be obtained, or a very considerable Time allow'd to make up and dispose of our present Stocks.

Notes

Chapter 2

1. Anne Ward, "Quilting in the North of England," *Folk Life* (Cardiff, Wales), Vol. 4 (1966), p. 75.
2. Averil Colby, *Quilting* (New York: Charles Scribner's Sons, 1971), pp. 5-6.
3. Margaret E. Grimes, ed., *Les Lais del Desiré,* in Averil Colby, *Patchwork* (London: B. T. Batsford Ltd., 1958), p. 22. For references to quilts in medieval times, see *The Oxford English Dictionary* (London: Oxford University Press, 1933), entry under "quilt." From 1290, in England, there is this: "Maketh a bed . . . of quoiltene and of materasz." From the *Romance of Sir Beves of Hamtoun,* of 1320: "Foure hondred beddes of silk echon, Quiltes of gold thar upon." From *Merlin or the Early History of King Arthur,* 1450: "Thei lay down to slepe upon the grass for other quyltes ne pilowes hadde thei noon." And this from 1489: "Coytes or matrases or sacques."
4. Colby, *Quilting,* p. 19.
5. *Ibid.*
6. Patricia Wardle, *Guide to English Embroidery* (A Victoria and Albert Museum booklet; London: Her Majesty's Stationery Office, 1970), p. 9 .
7. *Ibid.*
8. A few examples, extracted from Welsh household inventories: "Item a quylte of redd sylke In the Nursery . . . Item a quylte and a coverlet of dornes" (1551). "Item ij old quiltes of yellowe sercnet . . . Item a changeable silke quilt . . . Item an old black and white silk quilt for a bedd . . ." (1592). For further examples, see Mavis FitzRandolph, *Traditional Quilting* (London: B. T. Batsford Ltd., 1954), p. 16.
9. In this system a mordant, a fixing agent, is applied to the cloth, then the material goes to the dye bath and the dye reacts chemically with the mordant forming a permanent solution, a color in the cloth. For a complete account of this process, see: John Irwin and Katharine Brett, *Origins of Chintz* (London: Her Majesty's Stationery Office, 1970); and Alice Baldwin Beer, *Trade Goods: A Study of Indian Chintz in the Collection of the Cooper-Hewitt Museum of Decorative Arts and Design* (Washington: Smithsonian Institution Press, 1970).
10. This correspondence is from a company factor in Surat, 1609: "Pintadoes of all sorts, especially the finest, as it seemeth to me, should yield good profit, I mean such as are for quilts and for fine hangings. Quilts made both of white calicoes and of all sorts of painted stuff are to be had in abundance, and very reasonable . . ." (Beer, *Trade Goods,* p. 24). In 1613 "Pintatho Carpetts" were sold by the Company in London (Irwin and Brett, *Origins of Chintz,* p. 16). "In 1618 John Browne wrote the London company from Ahmedabad: 'For these quilts party-cullered, we shall by Godes grace make tryall for their provision according to your order in some small quantitie, and those also of cuttaine but no great number for that we cannot get taylors enough to work' " (Beer, *Trade Goods,* p. 26). The following year this correspondence, giving specifications for desired quilts, passed between factors in India: ". . . some, all of one kind chinte, the lynings and uper parts of one and the same; . . . and some to have borders only of different cullers about a covide deep, to hange by the bed side on all sides alike. This last is most used in India, and wee thinke will be most pleasinge to England. . . . They must be a little thicker and stronger sticht than ordinary, for their better lastinge. . . . His Lordship had three or four which he bought lasker sticht with cullered silke, that will give good contente in England . . ." (Beer, *Trade Goods,* p. 26).
11. Irwin and Brett, *Origins of Chintz,* p. 27.
12. *Ibid.,* pp. 3-4.
13. For two examples, see *Origins of Chintz,* p. 28.
14. Daniel DeFoe, "A Plan of the English Commerce" (1728), in Edward Baines, *History of the Cotton Manufacture in Great Britain* (London: H. Fisher and P. Jackson, 1835), p. 80.
15. Wardle, *Guide to English Embroidery,* p. 20.
16. Daniel DeFoe, "A Brief State of the Question between the Printed and Painted Callicoes, and the Woollen and Silk Manufacture" (London: 1719) in Irwin and Brett, *Origins of Chintz,* p. 33.
17. Wardle, *Guide to English Embroidery,* p. 20.
18. Irwin and Brett, *Origins of Chintz,* p. 33.
19. Quoted in Agnes Miall, *Patchwork Old and New,* Woman's Magazine Handbook No. 1 (London: The Woman's Magazine Office, 1937), p. 18.
20. Colby, *Patchwork,* p. 96.

Chapter 3

1. The "Great Ship," bound for the colonies, was lost at sea in 1646. Listed in the wills of those aboard were "down and feather beds with curtains and bedding . . . a canopy bed with feather bedding, curtains and valance." Elizabeth Wells Robertson, *American Quilts,* (New York: The Studio Publications Inc., 1948), p. 13.
2. George Francis Dow, *The Arts and Crafts in New England: 1704-1775* (Topsfield, Massachusetts: Wayside Press, 1927), p. 154.
3. *Ibid.,* p. 159.
4. *Ibid.,* p. 160.
5. *Ibid.,* p. 71.
6. Doubtless there were also among them Indian quilts, for

the colonists wished to be in fashion and another importation was the rage for Indian materials. In the Boston *News-Letter* for August 6-13, 1716, there was an ad for "Indian Counterpanes," and in the same paper for June 5-17, 1740, one finds advertised "India Pictures" (palampores?) (Dow, *Arts and Crafts of New England,* p. 159). A Virginia household inventory of 1698 lists "a feather-bed, one sett Kitterminster curtains," (the same "Kidderminster" as in "The Case of the Quilt-Makers," see the Appendix) "and Vallens bedstead . . ." (Maud Wilder Goodwin, *The Colonial Cavalier,* New York: Lovell, Coryell and Co., 1894, p. 28). Lionel Chute, a schoolmaster in New England in the seventeenth century, had an "old damskell coverlet" for his bed, while some neighbors enjoyed "branched and embroider coverlets" (palampores again?) and a "coverlet made of tapestry" (George Francis Dow, *Domestic Life in New England in the Seventeenth Century,* Topsfield, Mass.: Perkins Press, 1925, p. 21). An aggrieved householder advertised in the Boston *Gazette* for December 20-27, 1736, for his stolen bedcover, ". . . a Damask Counterpin of a bed, one breadth, marked S.P. with a red and purple chintz border: from a Yard near Fort Hill, Boston. 20s Reward " (Dow, *Arts and Crafts in New England,* p. 157). It is impossible to tell, of course, which if any of these bedcovers were made in the colonies.

7. Goodwin, *The Colonial Cavalier,* p. 56.
8. Dow, *Arts and Crafts in New England,* p. 154.
9. A number of writers have attributed the genesis of the patchwork quilt in America to Dutch and English settlers, weight usually given the Puritan stock of the latter. While it may well be true, there is more romantic speculation than sound evidence supporting it. The general approach has been something like this: the Puritans found themselves on an inhospitable shore with few resources and little recourse to supply from Europe. As the stores they brought with them were used up, and the hard winters pressed upon them, they turned to salvaging whatever they could in the way of textile scraps, and, anxious to make the fullest use of them, pieced together from these scraps, "crazy"-style or random-patterned quilts.

Doubtless the Puritans patched, and doubtless they put materials together, a practice current among those in need in every culture which has textiles. But there is no substantiation for the notion that the random-style quilt was the first made here. It is equally likely that they used skins for bed coverings as their quilts wore out, and waited for the infrequent ships from Europe for more supplies of cloth and perhaps ready-made quilts. "Wool . . . was scarce and precious, and when the garments they brought with them could be 'clouted' no more, leather from the skins of wild animals and especially deerskin in the Indian style were called into service to make new ones" (Stearns, *Homespun and Blue,* New York: Charles Scribner's Sons, 1940, p. 8). In any case the emphasis on the Puritans in many histories of quiltmaking overlooks the other contemporaneous settlements we have discussed, and the possibility that the first quilts made in the New World were sewn by Dutch housewives in New Amsterdam, or the wives and servants of planters in Virginia.

10. Dow, *Arts and Crafts in New England,* p. 273.
11. "Joshua Hempstead of New London, Connecticut . . . farmer, carpenter, trader, justice, man of affairs in the town, recorded in his diary many homely details of the textile operations and transactions in his household. Serge made in the house in 1716 was sent out to be finished. Coarse wool spun at home he took to a neighbor to be woven into coverlets. He purchased of another neighbor nine and a half yards of cloth, 'Ye neat produce of 4 sheep.' He had made for himself coats, jackets, or breeches of cherryderry, camblet, oznaburg, calimanco, duffel, and stuff. He took to a spinner wool to be made into worsted yarn and to be spun for mixed (blue and white or gray and white) stocking yarn. He went to a weaver with a web to be woven for his son's suit and took away with him a bedtick just off the loom. He lent out his old feather bed, a tow sheet, a striped blanket, and a white bed rug. He exchanged linen for wool, wool for linen, yarn for tow, raw wool for 'scotch cloth' " (Catherine Fennelly, *Textiles in New England: 1790-1840,* Sturbridge Village Booklet Series, 1961, p. 4).
12. A Massachusetts will of 1656 listed "painted Callico Curtains and Valiants" (Irwin and Brett, *Origins of Chintz,* p. 25). Margarita Van Varick's will, set down in 1695 in New York, lists "one Chint flowered carpet; one callico carpet; . . . one Chint petticote, one callico waistcoat, one Chint ditto . . ." (Beer, *Trade Goods,* p. 35). Margarita Van Varick's will also included: ". . . a pss of Chints and remnant of Chints . . ."—"these two," as Alice Beer remarked in her *Trade Goods,* "deemed worth leaving to two sons . . ." (Beer, *Trade Goods,* p. 35).
13. Montgomery, *Printed Textiles,* p. 46.
14. Woodrow Wilson, *A History of the American People* (New York: Harper and Brothers, 1906), Vol. II, p. 123 and p. 173. See also Montgomery, *Printed Textiles,* p. 46.
15. Speaking of the troubles of Hamilton Rowan, who established a calico printing and dyeing business on the Brandywine River in the last years of the eighteenth century, Mrs. Montgomery mentions: " 'Riders,' or salesmen, informed the merchants that accounts would be payable forthwith if American printed textiles were discovered on their shelves along with British goods" (Montgomery, *Printed Textiles,* p. 101).
16. Fennelly, *Textiles in New England,* p. 23.
17. Marshall Davidson, *The American Heritage History of American Antiques from the Revolution to the Civil War* (New York: American Heritage Publishing Co., 1968), p. 10.
18. Rectangles are one of the most commonly used forms in piecing because of the convenience of fitting together forms which are cut to right angles.

19. A further illustration of the multiple possibilities of a single
     block design is in the two Drunkard's Path quilts
     illustrated, one showing its use as the design for an entire
     quilt, the other showing the effect of multiple blocks of that
     same image joined together.
     Left: A single block used for an entire top. Such large-scale
     use of a block is quite unusual, though merely a logical
     extension of the normal scaling up-or-down process each
     quiltmaker went through when designing her work.
     (Courtesy of George Schoellkopf)
     Right: Here the pattern in its more usual conformation, a
     number of blocks linked to form an overall pattern.
     (Rhea Goodman, The Quilt Gallery, Inc.)

Chapter 4

1. (opposite page).
    Several other stereoscope cards showing quilts in period
    settings. The photograph on the left shows a children's
    version of a quilting bee, gossip and all. On the right, a
    Wild Goose Chase quilt is folded—ready for the doll. The
    next two show American quilts of the late 1890s: lower
    right, a fine stylized Basket pattern; lower left, an Irish
    Chain. (America Hurrah Antiques, N.Y.C.)

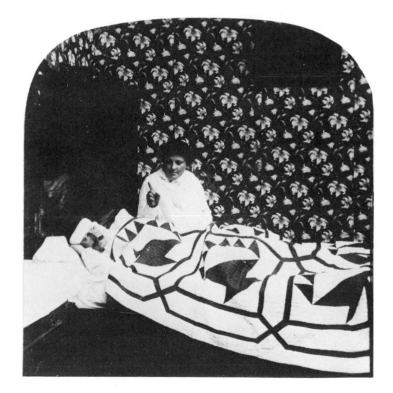

2. A watercolor, by Benjamin Harrison, shows the fair held by the American Institute for the City of New York (c. 1845), a society to promote the domestic and manufactured arts. Hanging above cases stocked with furnishings typical of the time, and below an upper gallery crowded in the "picture" gallery manner of the period with what appear to be prints and drawings, are a frieze of quilts running down both sides of the room. Some are ornate appliqués. Others are simple geometric patterns; one can recognize the Variable Star, one of the oldest of quilt designs, the Irish Chain, and other well-known patterns. Such evidence indicates both the ubiquitousness of the pieced quilt in the American scene, and the sharp contrast between such quilts and the prevailing decorative taste of the time.

3. Herwin Schaefer, *Nineteenth Century Modern: The Functional Tradition in Victorian Design* (New York: Praeger, 1970). See also John Kouwenhoven, *Made in America* (New York: Doubleday, 1948); Siegfried Giedion, *Mechanization Takes Command: A Contribution to Anonymous History* (New York, Oxford University Press, 1948).

4. For example, the American axe, that essential pioneer tool, had by the nineteenth century developed from the heavy, straight-handled, straight-edged iron form of ancient lineage, brought with the first settlers, into the elegantly proportioned and efficient steel tool described in a "Handbook for Settlers in the United States," published in Frankfurt in 1848. "Its curved cutting edge, its heavier head, counterbalanced by the handle, gives the axe greater power at its swing, facilitates its penetration, reduces the expenditure of human energy, speeds up the work. . . . The handle of the axe is curved, whereby it is more easily guided and forcibly swung. . ." In comparison, the nineteenth century European axe "had hardly changed since late Gothic times . . ." (Giedion, *Mechanization Takes Command*, p. 147).

5. Dow, *Domestic Life in New England in the Seventeenth Century*.

6. Agnes Miall, an English writer, on the subject, saw the development of the block system as a condition of the westward pioneer movement, saying: ". . . American women evolved the sort of design which could be pieced in separate small squares that were afterwards joined together into a larger top. . ." (Agnes Miall, *Patchwork Old and New*, p. 130). However, Mrs. Miall's implication that American women "evolved" the block style in response to the conditions of pioneer life is not historically substantiated. But certainly it was a working form which was amenable to those conditions, and which as a consequence they used and developed. It was a style suited to the quick production of necessary bedcovers, utility quilts, from limited available material, in contrast to the more "elegant" appliquéd and pieced high-style quilts.

7. *Godey's Lady's Book*. Philadelphia: 1830-1898.

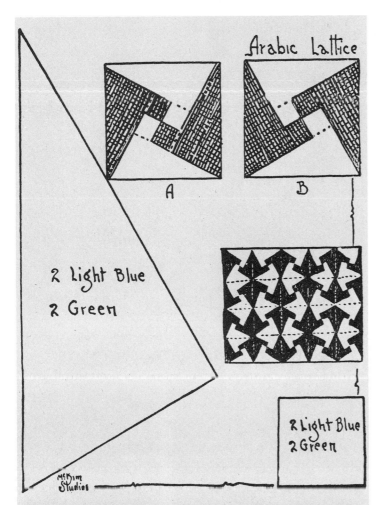

ARABIC LATTICE

FOR those who want something different again and who do not mind fitting around corners to achieve the results we suggest "Arabic Lattice." The originator of this old pattern must have had a flair for the romantic as witnessed by the name as well as an aptitude for work, as the little blocks are really difficult to piece.

Each finishes 5½ inches square if seams are allowed extra and they must be pieced in A and B style to set together alternately for the all-over pattern. These blocks in a continuing row turn an intriguing corner as well as making a single repeat border that is most effective.

A pieced center of 30 or 42 little blocks, within a wide band of plain color for fancy quilting, then a pieced border and a plain to finish would make a stunning quilt.

Material Estimate: Forty-two of the 5½-inch blocks would finish into a center about 33x38 inches—6 blocks wide by 7 long. This center plus a 12-inch border of light blue, then a 5½-inch pieced border, and last a 3-inch border of green, will make the completed quilt top 74x79 inches. This requires 5 yards of light blue and 4½ yards of green, or a total of 9½ yards of material.

For the intricately pieced center, lay out in straight lines for quilting and repeat the Tulip or Snowflakes designs for quilting the wide plain border.

(Reproduced from Ruby Short McKim's *One Hundred and One Patchwork Patterns,* p. 87. Courtesy of Dover Publications.)

8. Ruby Short McKim, *One Hundred and One Patchwork Patterns* (New York: Dover Publications, 1968) p. 87.

9. In an account printed in *House Beautiful* of an encounter between the writer and an aged spinster in her Tennessee cabin, there is this description of the origins of a pattern:

"Mother," said the spinster, "had fourteen children, but only my brother lived. Some did not live long enough to be named; but there were two, twins, that lived a week, and she named them Rose and Roselle. I think she grieved for them, more than for all the others. They were buried in coffins dug out of pine logs—I heard her tell many a time how she lined the coffins with oak leaves.

"The field was plowed up the new year, and she lost track of their graves; they didn't have money for burying stones in those days, you know, and she wanted to keep them in mind somehow, so she made up a pattern of the twin roses" ("Patchwork Romance," *House Beautiful,* January 10, 1919, p. 24).

10. Stuart Robinson, *A History of Printed Textile* (London: Studio Vista Ltd., 1969), p. 7.

11. Florence Montgomery says of the new technology: "With the increased technical and chemical facility attained in the second half of the eighteenth century, printers were freed to achieve patterns of high aesthetic quality, but in the 1820s new mineral dyes and the greatly accelerated speed with which cloth could be printed in many colors loosed a flood of commercially acceptable prints—lively, gay, and novel but, to our eyes, all too often lacking in harmony of color, design, and motif" (Montgomery, *Printed Textiles,* p. 35). Mrs. Montgomery is not alone in mourning the passing of the earlier printed textiles; but it was precisely the strong colors, the gaiety—and cheapness—of the new fabrics which commended them to American quiltmakers, and helped cause that surge of quiltmaking during the latter part of the nineteenth century.

12. Giedion, *Mechanization Takes Command,* p. 345.

13. Schaefer, *Nineteenth Century Modern,* p. 66.

14. *Godey's,* Vol. 54, (Jan. 1857), p. 72. In March 1860, *Godey's* said: "Patchwork has especially established for itself the character of a winter industry, as it requires no additional light for its execution, the work which produces it being slight and easy. The only care which it exacts is a mathematical precision in the foundation shapes of which it is composed, and a knowledge of the laws of colors: that is, light and shade, and contrast. When these two points are remembered and practiced in the arrangement of patchwork, the ornamental effects may be produced" (*Godey's,* Vol. 60, March 1860, pp. 262-263).

15. "The Career of a Crazy Quilt," in *Godey's,* described the trials of a young girl of means and her friend trying to get together the requisite amount of silk scraps for a crazy quilt. They evolve elaborate schemes to obtain sample patches from material stores.

One girl's fiancé said: "Good Heavens, Marie! You are not going to make one of those abominable things, are you?'' ''I am going to make a crazy quilt, if that is what you mean,'' I said stiffly. ''I am sorry for that,'' he exclaimed. ''But I hope you won't make yourself a bore to your friends, Marie, as some girls do. I don't want to see you plaguing men for their old neckties, and all that sort of thing.'' ''I hope I know what is becoming to a lady,'' I said, with crushing emphasis. ''But you won't do that, will you, Marie?'' he persisted. ''Promise me you won't. You don't know how the fellows make fun of these girls that go around begging for old silk—'ragpickers' they call them.''

In the end, of course, she makes the quilt, and keeps the boy. His good sense was hardly the norm (*Godey's,* Vol. 109, July 1884, p. 36).

16. *Godey's,* Vol. 106 (May 1883), p. 462.
17. *Godey's,* Vol. 106 (April 1883), p. 371.
18. *Godey's,* Vol. 42 (November 1851), p. 198.
19. *Arthur's Home Magazine,* October 1883, p. 304.
20. Earl Robacker, *Touch of the Dutchland* (New York: A. S. Barnes and Co., 1965), p. 83.
21. *Demorest's Monthly Magazine,* August 1867.
22. Ralph McGinnis, *The Good Old Days* (New York: Harper, 1960), p. 63.

Chapter 5

1. Frances Lichten, *Folk Art of Rural Pennsylvania* (New York: Charles Scribner's Sons, 1946), p. 168.
2. T. S. Arthur, ''The Quilting Party,'' *Godey's,* Vol. 39 (September 1849), p. 185.
3. Kathryne Hall Travis, ''Quilts of the Ozarks,'' in *Southwest Review,* Vol. 1 (January 1930).
4. John Hostetler, *Amish Society* (Baltimore: The Johns Hopkins Press, 1963), pp. 161-162.
5. Travis, ''Quilts of the Ozarks,'' pp. 240-241.
6. *Ibid.*
7. Lichten, *Folk Art of Rural Pennsylvania,* p. 167.
8. Travis, ''Quilts of the Ozarks,'' p. 242. Women of every class were expected to be proficient with the needle; in *The Arts and Crafts in New York—1726-1776* there is reprinted this advertisement from the New York *Mercury,* May 6, 1765: ''Mrs. Carroll proposes teaching young Ladies plain work, Samplars, French Quilting, knoting for Bed Quilts or Toilets, Dresden, flowering on Cat Gut, shading (with silk or Worsted) on Cambrick, Lawn or Holland'' (Rita S. Gottesman, *The Arts and Crafts in New York, 1726-1776,* New York: New-York Historical Society, 1938, p. 276). Similar advertisements of the period ran in other cities, and sewing was a part of the curriculum of girls' schools from the eighteenth and well into the nineteenth century. This advertisement, in the Philadelphia *American Weekly Mercury* for March 5, 1728, is typical: ''A boarding school, also Reading, Writing, Cyphering, Dancing and several sorts of Needlework, at the house of George Brownell, Second-Street, Philadelphia'' (Margaret B. Schiffer, *Historical Needlework of Pennsylvania,* New York: Bonanza Books, p. 21) .

    Godey's in May of 1860 considered it ''a matter of chief importance . . . every Board of Education [should] see that the needle has its place with the pen in every public school, where the children of the poor seem to be taught everything but what will help them when they come to the struggle for life. Mothers who have themselves buried this disused talent, should remember that strange reverses and unforeseen misfortunes may come upon the petted daughter, reared in luxurious indolence, and at best, it is like setting her out on a voyage of life, as wife and mother, with her hands helpless to steer the little barque clear of innumerable obstacles, even if she is so fortunate as to escape rocks and breakers'' (*Godey's,* Vol. 60, May 1860, p. 45).
9. *Godey's,* Vol. 48 (Feb. 1854), p. 127.
10. *Godey's,* Vol. 51 (Aug. 1855), pp. 1-5.
11. Kouwenhoven, *Made in America,* p. 42.
12. *Godey's,* Vol. 61 (Sept. 1860), p. 271.
13. *Scientific American,* March 18, 1892.
14. Daisy Pat Stockwell, *Land of the Oldest Hills* (Caxton, Ohio: Caxton Printers Ltd., 1957), p. 74.
15. Lichten, *Folk Art of Rural Pennsylvania,* p. 172.
16. Ruth Finley, *Old Patchwork Quilts* (Newton Centre, Mass.: Charles T. Branford Co., 1970) .
17. *Ibid.,* p. 103.
18. American designs evidently were also exported. *The Dictionary of Needlework,* published in London in 1882, referring to the Log Cabin block under the heading ''American Patchwork,'' describes it as ''a work well known in Canada under the name of Loghouse Quilting, but only lately introduced to England.'' (Sophia Frances Anne Caulfield and Blance C. Saward, *The Dictionary of Needlework,* New York: Arno Press, 1972).
19. Alice Earle, *Home Life in Colonial Days* (New York: The Macmillan Co., 1917).
20. *Ibid.*
21. Fennelly, *Textiles in New England,* pp. 9-12.
22. Professional quilters in England took from three days to two weeks to quilt an average-sized cover. Quiltmaking was a distinct part of the rural tradition in northern England and Wales, with some similarities to American practices. Though pieced quilts were made there, emphasis was more on fine quilting of plain whole-cloth quilts. ''The girls of the family all helped in making quilts,'' said a Welshwoman, ''and as each was married she had all she needed. They were an important part of a girl's dowry; six seems to have been the usual allowance in Wales.'' Welsh ladies also worked together in quilting, ''making a quilt for each in turn'' (FitzRandolph , *Traditional Quilting,* pp. 32-33). This was, however, considered bad form by the professional quilters whose livelihood depended on the work. Often these professionals were itinerant, traveling from farm to farm and living there while they did the

season's quilting. Sometimes an apprentice worked with them. There were also professional quiltmarkers, who stenciled or drew their original designs for quilting on tops brought to them, a practice also followed in the colonial period in the United States. Ruth Finley mentions the 1747 advertisement in Boston of "Sara Hunt, dwelling in the House of James Nichols in School Street," who "stamped counterpins, curtains, linens and cottons for quilting" (Finley, *Old Patchwork Quilts,* p. 142).

23. Lichten, *Folk Art of Rural Pennsylvania,* pp. 172-175.
24. Elias Nason, "A New England Village Quilting Party in the Olden Times," *Granite Monthly,* Vol. 8 (1885), p. 235.
25. *Ibid.*
26. *Ibid.,* pp. 235-236.
27. McGinnis, *The Good Old Days,* p. 63 .
28. Josiah's Wife Allen, "The Quilting at Miss Jones's," in *Godey's,* Vol. 77 (July 1868), p. 43.
29. Travis, "Quilts of the Ozarks," p. 239.
30. FitzRandolph, *Traditional Quilting,* p. 84.
31. Lichten, *Folk Art of Rural Pennsylvania,* p. 170.
32. *Ibid.,* p. 168.
33. *Ibid.*
34. *Ibid.*
35. Phebe Earle Gibbons, *Pennsylvania Dutch and Other Essays* (Philadelphia: J. B. Lippincott, 1872), pp. 33-35.
36. Lichten, *Folk Art of Rural Pennsylvania,* p. 226.
37. Finley, *Old Patchwork Quilts,* p. 38
38. Gibbons, *Pennsylvania Dutch and Other Essays.*

Chapter 6

1. Sam Hunter, *American Painting of the Twentieth Century* (New York: Harry N. Abrams), p. 350.
2. Thomas Hess, *Abstract Painting* (New York: The Viking Press, 1951), p. 530.
3. *Ibid.,* pp. 56-57.
4. Barbara Rose has pointed out the influence of the context of art objects on such artists as Jasper Johns and Robert Rauschenberg (Barbara Rose, *American Art Since 1900: A Critical History,* New York: Praeger Publishers, 1967), the latter of whom illustrated this in *The Bed,* in which a Courthouse Steps quilt serves as the main element in a large mixed media painting. The quilt was taken from a bed, where it had no doubt served to warm sleeping householders. Were they all-unsuspecting sleeping under "art," or did the quilt become that only when Rauschenberg made his bed on the wall? Thus stated, the answer would have to be that Rauschenberg made the quilt into art by incorporating it in his painting, even though the quilt itself, extracted and put on the wall, would, like many of its fellows, be visually similar to paintings of some of Rauschenberg's contemporaries.
5. Hess, *Abstract Painting,* p. 400.
6. Adam Heath, *Abstract Painting: Its Origin and Meaning* (London: A. Tiranti, 1953).
7. Alan Solomon, *Towards a New Abstraction* (Catalogue of an exhibition at the Jewish Museum, New York, 1963), p. 20.

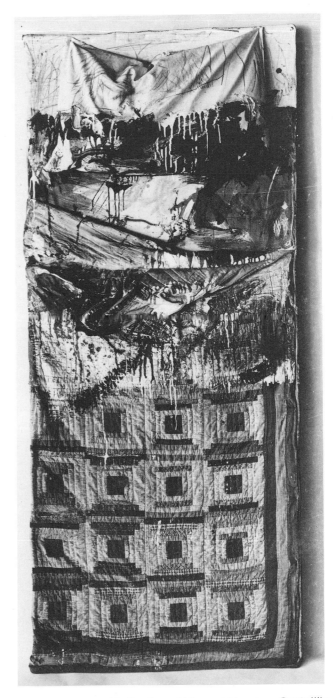

(Collection of Mr. and Mrs. Leo Castelli)

Bibliography

Andrews, Charles M. *Colonial Folkways: A Chronicle of American Life in the Reign of the Georges.* New Haven, Connecticut: Yale University Press, 1919.

Baines, Edward. *History of the Cotton Manufacture in Great Britain.* London: H. Fisher, R. Fisher, and P. Jackson, 1835.

Beer, Alice Baldwin. *Trade Goods, A Study of Indian Chintz in the Collection of the Cooper-Hewitt Museum of Decorative Arts and Design, Smithsonian Institute.* Washington, D.C.: Smithsonian Institution Press, 1970.

Carlisle, Lilian Baker. *Pieced Work and Appliqué Quilts at Shelburne Museum.* Museum Pamphlet Series, Number 2. Shelburne, Vermont: The Shelburne Museum, 1957.

Caulfield, Sophia Frances, and Saward, Blanche C. *The Dictionary of Needlework.* New York: Arno Press, Inc., 1972.

Colby, Averil. *Patchwork.* London: B. T. Batsford Ltd.; Newton Centre, Massachusetts: Charles T. Branford Co., 1958.

Colby, Averil. *Patchwork Quilts.* New York: Charles Scribner's Sons, 1965.

Colby, Averil. *Quilting.* New York: Charles Scribner's Sons, 1971.

Constantine, Mildred, and Drexler, Arthur. *The Object Transformed.* Museum of Modern Art Catalogue for that exhibition. New York: Museum of Modern Art, 1966.

Davidson, Marshall B. *The American Heritage History of American Antiques from the Revolution to the Civil War.* New York: American Heritage Publishing Co., Inc., 1968.

Davidson, Mildred. *American Quilts.* Chicago: The Art Institute of Chicago, 1966.

Denton, William Bush, Jr. *Old Quilts.* Maryland: Privately printed, 1946.

Dow, George Francis. *The Arts and Crafts in New England: Gleanings from Boston Newspapers.* Topsfield, Massachusetts: Wayside Press, 1927.

Dow, George Francis. *Domestic Life in New England in the Seventeenth Century.* Topsfield, Massachusetts: Perkins Press, 1925.

Dunham, Lydia Roberts. "Denver Art Museum Quilt Collection." The Denver Art Museum Winter Quarterly, 1963.

Fennelly, Catherine. *Textiles in New England.* Sturbridge, Massachusetts: Old Sturbridge Village Booklet Series, 1961.

Finley, Ruth. *Old Patchwork Quilts and the Women Who Made Them.* Newton Centre, Massachusetts: Charles T. Branford Co., 1971.

FitzRandolph, Mavis. *Traditional Quilting.* London: B. T. Batsford, 1954.

Garside, Frances. "Patchwork Romance," *House Beautiful,* (January 10, 1919), p. 24.

Giedion, Siegfried. *Mechanization Takes Command: A Contribution to Anonymous History.* New York: Oxford University Press, 1948.

Godey's Magazine and Lady's Book. Philadelphia: 1830-1898.

Goodwin, Maud Wilder. *The Colonial Cavalier.* New York: Lovell, Coryell & Co., 1894.

Gottesman, Rita S. *The Arts and Crafts in New York—1726-1776.* Collections of the New-York Historical Society for the Year 1936. New York: Published for NYHS, 1938.

Greenough, Horatio. *The Travels, Observations, and Experience of a Yankee Stonecutter.* Florida: Gainesville, 1882.

Hake, Elizabeth. *English Quilting Old and New.* London: B. T. Batsford, Ltd., 1937.

Hall, Carrie A., and Kretsinger, Rose G. *The Romance of the Patchwork Quilt in America.* New York: Bonanza Books, 1935.

Heath, Adrian. *Abstract Painting: Its Origins and Meaning.* London: A. Tiranti, 1953.

Hess, Thomas. *Abstract Painting.* New York: The Viking Press, 1951.

Hinson, Dolores A. *Quilting Manual.* New York: Hearthside Press, Inc., 1966.

Hostetler, John. *Amish Society.* Baltimore: The Johns Hopkins Press, 1963.

Hunter, Sam. *American Painting of the Twentieth Century.* New York: Harry N. Abrams, Inc., 1972.

Ickis, Marguerite. *The Standard Book of Quilt Making and Collecting.* New York: Dover Publications, Inc., 1959.

Irwin, John, and Brett, Katharine B. *Origins of Chintz.* London: Her Majesty's Stationery Office, 1970.

Jourdain, M. *English Secular Embroidery.* London: Kegan Paul, Trench, Trubner & Co., 1910.

Kirk, John T. *Early American Furniture.* New York: Alfred A. Knopf, 1970.

Kouwenhoven, John. *Made in America.* New York: Doubleday, 1948.

Laury, Jean Ray. *Quilts and Coverlets.* New York: Van Nostrand-Reinhold Co., 1970.

Lichten, Frances. *Folk Art of Rural Pennsylvania.* New York: Charles Scribner's Sons, 1946.

McGinnis, Ralph. *The Good Old Days.* New York: Harper, 1960.

McKim, Ruby Short. *One Hundred and One Patchwork Patterns.* New York: Dover Publications, Inc., 1962.

Miall, Agnes M. *Patchwork Old and New.* Woman's Magazine Handbook No. 1 (London: The Woman's Magazine Office, 1937).

Miller, Nora. *The Girl in the Rural Family.* North Carolina: University of North Carolina Press, 1935.

Montgomery, Florence M. *Printed Textiles: English and American Cottons and Linens 1700-1850.* (A Winterthur Book) New York: The Viking Press, 1970.

Nason, Elias. "A New England Village Quilting Party in the Olden Times." *Granite Monthly,* Vol. 8 (1885), pp. 235-239.

Percival, MacIver. *The Chintz Book.* London: Wm. Heineman Ltd., 1923.
Peto, Florence. *American Quilts and Coverlets.* New York: Chanticleer Press, 1949.
Peto, Florence. *Historic Quilts.* New York: The American Historical Co., Inc., 1939.
Pritchard, Mabel Wentworth. *Country Echoes.* New York: Comet Press Books, 1955.

Robacker, Earl F. *Touch of the Dutchland.* New York: A. S. Barnes and Co., Inc., 1965.
Robertson, Elizabeth Wells. *American Quilts.* New York: The Studio Publications, Inc., 1948.
Robinson, Stuart. *A History of Printed Textiles.* London: Studio Vista, 1969.
Rose, Barbara. *American Art Since 1900: A Critical History.* New York: Praeger Publishers, 1967.

Safford, Carleton L., and Bishop, Robert. *America's Quilts and Coverlets.* New York: E. P. Dutton & Co., Inc., 1972.
Schaefer, Herwin. *Nineteenth Century Modern.* New York: Praeger Publishers, Inc., 1970.
Schiffer, Margaret B. *Historical Needlework of Pennsylvania.* New York: Charles Scribner's Sons, 1968.
Scott, Beatrice. *The Craft of Quilting in the North Country.* Leicester: Dryad Press, 1928.
Seuphor, Michel. *Abstract Painting.* London: Prentice-Hall International, 1962.
Solomon, Alan. *Towards a New Abstraction.* New York: Jewish Museum, 1963.
Stearns, Martha Genung. *Homespun and Blue: A Study of American Crewel Embroidery.* New York: Charles Scribner's Sons, 1963.
Stockwell, Daisy Pat. *Land of the Oldest Hills.* Ohio: Caxton Printers Ltd., 1957.
Stoudt, John Joseph. *Early Pennsylvania Arts and Crafts.* New York: A. S. Barnes and Co., 1964.

Travis, Kathryne Hall. "Quilts of the Ozarks." *Southwest Review,* Vol. 1 (Dallas, Texas: S.M.U.) , January 1930.

Victoria and Albert Museum. *Notes on Quilting.* London: Her Majesty's Stationery Office, 1932.

Wardle, Patricia. *Guide to English Embroidery.* London: Her Majesty's Stationery Office, 1970.
White, Margaret. *Quilts and Counterpanes in the Newark Museum.* New Jersey: The Newark Museum, 1948.
Wooster, Ann-Sargent. *Quiltmaking: The Modern Approach to a Traditional Craft.* New York: Drake Publishers, Inc., 1972.

Index

Following page
Figure 43. Log cabin—light and dark
variation. Pennsylvania, c. 1910. 72″ x 72″.